THE DANCE OF THE FLYING GURNARDS

∽∾∽

THE DANCE OF THE
FLYING GURNARDS

⟨∾⟩

AMERICA'S COASTAL CURIOSITIES
AND BEACHSIDE WONDERS

JOHN WALDMAN

THE LYONS PRESS

Guilford, Connecticut
An Imprint of The Globe Pequot Press

Printed in the United States of America

1   3   5   7   9   10   8   6   4   2

Design by Claire Zoghb

ISBN 1-58574-368-2

The Library of Congress Cataloging-in-Publication Data is available on file.

In mare multa latent.
—Oppian

Many things are hidden in the sea.

For my barefoot companions,
Laura and Steve.

THE DANCE OF THE FLYING GURNARDS

∾∾

INTRODUCTION

The seashore has been called the earth's greatest meeting place, and the surf one of nature's finest edges. Against this setting—and including the surrounding bays, estuaries, and inshore ocean waters—a panoply of compelling natural events occur and spectacles can be seen. Some are rare, such as beaches that burn and finding valuable ambergris on the shore; some are frequent, such as fish that fly and night waters that glow with electric blue light. Some are subtle, like the annual "glass" eel invasion up rivers or the machinations of tide pool life; others are conspicuous, such as when horseshoe crab hordes storm the beach to spawn. Some are highly predictable, such as when grunion fish flop on California sands or Gulf Coast jubilees occur; some take the observer by surprise, such as loomings from beyond the horizon and the spooky lights of Saint Elmo's fire. And some are as endearing as watching dolphin or sea otters cavort; others are frightening—or even deadly: shark attacks, hurricanes, and tsunami. This book describes North American occurrences of these great and varied sea phenomena, a range that encompasses everything from the *slime* to the *sublime*.

This volume may be the first of its kind. Many, often terse, regional field guides exist to help identify marine plants and animals. Then there are personal narratives on long reaches of coastline by Rachel Carson, John Hay, George Reiger, and others, or on specific locations such as Cape Cod by Thoreau and Henry Beston. But until now, there has been no single sourcebook to the natural charms and menaces of the three North American shores—one that describes basic and surprising marine phenomena, celebrating what is ob-

servable by those who watch, touch, or float upon the sea. In
this book I have tried to infuse each topic with its lore, sci-
ence, and beauty, in the spirit of Steinbeck and Ricketts who
planned, but never completed, a seacoast guidebook whose
treatment "will revolt against the theory that only the dull is
accurate and only the tiresome, valuable."

The continental stage for this theater of the sea is enormous. Maritime Canada and British Columbia have almost
endlessly convoluted margins. The U.S. Atlantic coast alone
has a general shoreline of a little over two thousand miles,
but unwind its tidal bays, coves, and peninsulas, and it to-
tals many times that. Maine has the epitome of craggy
coastline; it measures only 230 miles end to end—but a line
tracing all of its inlets, coves, and bays spans about 3,500
miles. The Gulf of Mexico coast between Florida and Texas
doesn't look lengthy, yet its actual seaboard extends more
than seventeen thousand miles. And even the relatively
straight-edged coast between California and Washington is
comprised of 88,600 miles of tidal edge.

To help orient the coastally curious to a shoreline almost overwhelming in scale I present a personal cornucopia
of curiosities—a compilation of what I believe are the best
and most intriguing natural and naturally influenced phenomena the seaside has to offer. To provide some order,
where an event or spectacle occurs across regions, I introduce it clockwise around the continent, from the Canadian
Maritimes, to the Gulf of Mexico coast, to California, all the
way to Alaska. But it is not the purpose of this guide to provide addresses, directions to, or telephone numbers for the
sites it mentions; to do so would waste space and be dis-
tracting. Too many phenomena are too widespread, occurring across too many shores and coastal reaches, to provide
these kinds of details (and besides, contact information

becomes quickly outdated). But in today's information age, zeroing in on the logistical facts is not difficult, and may only require opening a regional guidebook or striking a few keys on the Internet.

No, the goal of my book is to both sensitize and energize the reader to myriad possibilities. For the nautically naive— to introduce the sea as an environment to experience wonder; for the more seasoned mariner—to explain and point toward phenomena perhaps you are only vaguely aware of and could encounter by simply broadening your gaze or, with a little effort, by deliberately seeking them out.

Beachcombers roam the shores both for material items and psychic rewards. Divers, bird-watchers, and whale-watchers survey the waters to glimpse their remarkable array of animals. Anglers cast their lines not only to catch fish but just to "be out there" in the wild. *Gunkholing* is an old term sailors use for poking around the coastline in small boats, purely for the adventure of it; in the Chesapeake, watermen call it *progging*. Regardless of how it's practiced or what it's called, exploring the sea is always an enriching experience, capable of great surprises. In a world in which pleasure is becoming increasingly digitized, our inshore waters offer a refuge of simple and timeless delights—and sometimes even marvels—for those willing to walk, wade, row, or sail.

❦❦❦

AMBERGRIS

"Now this ambergris is a very curious substance. . . ."
Ishmael in Moby-Dick

Over the centuries when whaling was a major industry, almost the entire animal was used for a motley array of products: oil for lamps and lubrication; baleen, or whalebone, for corsets, collars, and umbrellas; and meat for humans and animals. But the most valuable commodity typically wasn't part of a slaughtered whale. Instead, ambergris, a strange waxy substance, was sometimes found cast along the shore, far from the whale that produced it.

Ambergris is formed in the bowels of sperm whales when the hard beaks of the squid and cuttlefish they eat irritate the leviathans' intestinal lining, much as a sand grain acts as a nucleus for a pearl in an oyster. The waxy ambergris probably lessens or eliminates this irritation. A mass of ambergris may grow to hundreds of pounds inside the whale, but eventually it is evacuated, to ultimately drift upon some beach. The largest chunk of ambergris ever found weighed 1,003 pounds, but pieces may be as small as an egg. Sometimes an ambergris chunk was discovered inside a slaughtered whale; whalers often would look first for ambergris, knowing that if it was found, the financial success of the expedition was already assured.

Fresh ambergris is soft, black, and foul smelling—appearing distinctly unvaluable, if not repulsive. After floating in the sea for a time and being exposed to air, it often turns amber in color and emits a pleasant, seaweedlike odor. It also may be mottled in appearance and have an irregular shape with the external appearance of cauliflower. A key feature is the pointed beaks of squid and cuttlefish embedded in its surface.

But ambergris has unique chemical properties and was long recognized as being superb in fixing perfumes; because of this, at times it had a value greater than gold, as much as eightfold in 1948. A single drop of tincture of ambergris applied to paper and placed in a book remains fragrant after forty years, and once it's handled, the fingers may smell of it even after several days and washings. But this weird whale product has also been put to a variety of other services. In the Orient it was used as an aphrodisiac and spice for food and wine. For a time it was eaten with eggs for breakfast by the Dutch and English nobility; later it was combined with chocolate as a restorative. And during the Civil War era in the United States this "expensive and potent" product was used in mixed drinks.

Ambergris is most reliably found along the shores of the Indian Ocean—in 1295 Marco Polo reported beachcombing of ambergris on islands off the coast of India and Madagascar, and he appears to be the first Westerner to have drawn its connection with whales. Given the scarcity of sperm whales near North American shores, discovering a fragment of any size along its coasts would be a rare event. But a hefty chunk presumably carried from southern latitudes by the Kuroshio Current washed up on British Columbia's Queen Charlotte Islands in 1946, and ten years later a similar find of fifteen pounds sold for twenty-six thousand dollars.

BALD EAGLES

Rank cowards or coastal icons?

The national symbol isn't hard to find these days—bald eagles are coming back at a rapid pace from their 1960s nadir. And although these great birds are found across most of North America, as fish lovers, they are very much a presence along the food-rich coastlines. In Maine, for instance, two-thirds of the eagles live along the seashore despite the state's abundance of large inland lakes and rivers.

Bald eagles are more opportunistic than the almost exclusively live-fish-eating ospreys that sometimes share their haunts. Bald eagles scavenge happily—a trait pointed out by some who've questioned their prominence as national icon. Chief among the bird's doubters was Benjamin Franklin, who claimed that "... he is a bird of bad moral character, he does not get his living honestly, you may see him perched on some dead tree, where, too lazy to fish for himself, he watches the labor of the fishing-hawk, and when that diligent bird has at length taken a fish, and is bearing it to its nest for the support of his mate and young ones, the bald eagle pursues him and takes it from him." He went on to call the bald eagle a "rank coward" because it flees from the little kingbird. Still, the nation's forefathers were not much moved by Franklin's candidate, the turkey, and the image of the eagle remains ubiquitous.

But despite their eye-catching seven-foot wingspan, not long ago finding a bald eagle was difficult. The birds' decline began as a consequence of the general attitude of decades past when it was accepted that potential livestock predators such as wolves and eagles should be killed whenever possible (shepherds in particular have always taken a dim view of eagles). The payment of bounties for slaughtered eagles contributed to this mind-set; during the Civil War, Virginia offered a bounty on them simply because they were the symbol of the Union enemy!

In the 1960s reproductive failures occurred because of the eggshell-thinning effects of organochlorine pesticides, especially DDT. DDT was sprayed in copious amounts by local governments to control mosquitoes; people were so naive about its dangers that children danced in its fumes as it was sprayed from trucks in suburban streets. Years later grim reality caught up when Rachel Carson referred to it as the "elixir of death." Although these chemicals became widespread in the environment and were presumably incorporated at some levels in almost all organisms, their concentrations in animals multiplied farther along the food chain. Eagles and other birds of prey are at the apex of these pyramids, and they suffered more than creatures at lower levels. But DDT was banned from use in the United States in 1972, and the targets of bounties were reversed—the National Wildlife Federation offered substantial rewards for information leading to the conviction of eagle killers. And slowly the bald eagle recovered.

Bald eagles are quite common on Cape Breton Island; on a visit there I saw seven in a few days simply by chance. A particularly eagle-rich area is the island's sprawling inland saltwater lake, Bras d'Or. Maine has a goodly number on Mount Desert Island. At some mid-Atlantic locations bald eagles are especially visible after lakes freeze during winter, when they are forced to aggregate around scarce open-water feeding areas. Some of these sites are natural, such as along the central Hudson River where in 1997 a pair of eagles nested for the first time in about a hundred years. Today about fifty to seventy-five individuals can be seen along the Hudson in January and February, and more during harsh winters. On some other rivers bald eagles use the pools below large dams, where turbulent waters remain ice-free and fish are concentrated. Good lookout spots for eagles can be found on Connecticut's Housatonic River and at the Conowingo Dam on the Susquehanna River. In southern New Jersey try upper Delaware Bay and the Mullica River.

It's believed that the Chesapeake Bay once supported more than a thousand eagle nests. Today there are far fewer, but they are increasing, especially along the Potomac and Rappahannock Rivers. The Blackwater National Wildlife

Refuge on Maryland's Eastern Shore also is an important mid-Atlantic breeding area.

On the Gulf Coast, Louisiana is home to about 150 breeding pairs. Nesting birds arrive in late September and leave by early April, as soon as the young are fledged. In Washington State, the Skagit River Valley hosts up to 350 bald eagles each winter. Locals there are so enthused that on weekends, volunteers run four viewing stations and in February, a festival celebrating the birds is held. Alaska has gone far to accommodate them, having established the Chilkat Bald Eagle Preserve, a forty-eight-thousand-acre parcel of river bottomlands with waters that stay open in winter, allowing the eagles to continue fishing.

BARRACUDA

Razor-toothed torpedoes

The fearsome reputation of the great barracuda is based on a mixture of reality and fantasy. Yes, the long, dentally overendowed jaws of a big one can chop off a human arm, but these attacks—if it's fair to decipher a fish's intentions— are mistakes in the name of hunger.

A great barracuda feeds by remaining stationary or moving slowly and waiting for smaller fish to come into range. Unlike many predator fish that must swallow their prey whole and so must select prey that will fit their mouths, barracuda are not "gape limited" and can cut a large fish down to size. Built like a spear with a broad forked tail for propulsion, a barracuda shoots forward at speeds above forty miles per hour to sever its prey into pieces.

Unprovoked assaults by barracuda on humans of any size are exceedingly rare. In 1960 a free diver was attacked near Pompano Beach, Florida, and the resulting wounds to his wrist and knee required thirty-one stitches. And in 1997

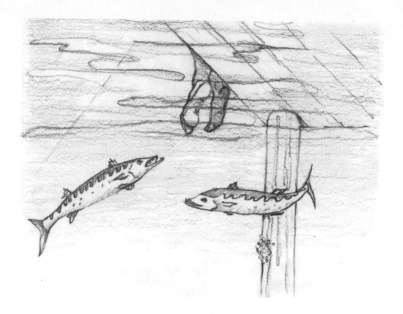

a woman cleaning the bottom of a boat in cloudy water was bitten by a barracuda. But even a small child swimming is not going to arouse the feeding instinct in a full-grown barracuda, which may stretch six feet and weigh fifty pounds. If a person wears jewelry or waves around some flashy object, however, the 'cuda may see it as a silvery baitfish, and then streak on the attack, jaws chopping, and inflict serious damage. They've also been known to charge shiny dive masks and scuba gear. The barracuda's bite, unlike the round, jagged wound of a shark, is straight and clean.

Great barracuda often hunt in the same shallows that people like to swim in. Moreover, they are exceedingly curious and may approach quite closely. I have snorkeled among them near a popular man-made reef on Florida's east coast and found the resident school to be unreactive, as if a person is something to be neither interested in nor afraid of. Nonetheless, the presence of such a formidable creature just a few feet away on its own territory makes for a compelling sight.

Great barracuda are a fine and often underrated gamefish. Anglers who seek them use wire between their lures and main line to prevent cutoffs from their razor teeth. It's common for fishermen landing other fish in barracuda-infested waters to—in the course of the battle—feel sudden extra weight on the line, followed by little resistance. Barracuda, like many other predators, are especially attracted to prey fish that are weak or in trouble in some way. A hooked fish is often sliced in half, with the front half continuing to be reeled in as the 'cuda makes off with the tail end—the angler being forced to settle for only the bleeding head of a grouper, snapper, or other victim.

Although there are other kinds of barracuda in the Atlantic and Pacific Oceans, the great barracuda of the Atlantic is the only threat to humans among them. Great barracuda are common in Florida waters and rare farther north.

∽∾∽

"BEACH DIAMONDS" AND OTHER SHORESIDE GEMSTONES

You won't get rich, but they're pretty

Diamond is a flattering term for a quartz crystal, but the energy of flowing water and the restless sea can burnish this commonplace mineral into a form approaching "a girl's best friend." The most reliable place to collect them is at Cape May, New Jersey. The Delaware River washes away pockets of quartz from higher terrain well upriver from the New Jersey shore. These crystals tumble downstream for thousands of years before they are entrained in the currents of Delaware Bay, often turning up at Cape May's Sunset Beach.

Most beach diamonds range from sand-grain to chicken-egg sized. The local Kechemeche Indians believed these stones held supernatural powers, bringing success and good fortune to the possessor. Today mineral enthusiasts enjoy polishing them further; when cut, they can closely resemble real diamonds. At Cape May the best hunting occurs after a storm in winter, when the rougher waters tend to deposit larger crystals.

Cape May's beach diamonds have West Coast analogues: Both jasper quartzes and semiprecious agates are found from California to British Columbia. Jade can be found at Jade Beach in California's Big Sur country. But Jade Beach is actually two beaches near the tiny towns of Lucia and Pacific Valley.

California's Pebble Beach, forty-five miles south of San Francisco, is famous for the beauty of its mineral makeup. The sea chips pebbles with delicate and captivating hues out of rock outcrops and casts them upon this beach. But collectors have so diminished this supply of stones that a halt has been placed on further collection.

Agate Beach near Arcata, California, attracts collectors, but by and large Oregon beaches are the best West Coast source of agates and other semiprecious stones; the periods right after winter storms yield the finest prospecting. Prized agate types include moonstone (brilliantly clear), moss (clear, but with mineral crystals), cloud (clear with dark formations), carmelian (bright red and translucent), and rainbow or iris (refracts seven iridescent colors). The rarest and most sought-after form is the water agate—a stone that has trapped in it a drop of water.

∞∞∞

BIOLUMINESCENCE
Unforgettable night swims

My father loved to swim at a popular beach in Long Island Sound, but mainly at night after the hordes of beachgoers had left. Part of the allure was the mystery of dark waters at a place that was not much different from a crowded pool in the daytime. Most exciting to my siblings, friends, and I who tagged along, however, was the sheer magic of being among small creatures that glowed as we waded or swam.

Years later I brought my own young children to a beach at dusk to introduce them to this phenomenon. They grew impatient as it slowly darkened, but when full blackness came, I carried them into the water and told them to stand still. Little was visible below the surface. Then I held them and swirled their legs around, creating vanishing meteor tails of electric blue light in the shallows. My children were delighted, splashing and plunging in an impromptu neon dance, and, although the air and water were chilly, they couldn't get enough of their firsthand encounter with bioluminescence.

Bioluminescence is the biological production of light. Not white-hot burning incandescence—it is miracle enough that creatures can glow at all—but rather a cool blue electric kind of light of low wattage but great beauty. Many kinds of animals generate this "living light," including certain sharks and other fish, squid, starfish, and crustaceans. Bioluminescence is closely associated with deep-sea animals that live in total darkness; the pioneering oceanographer William Beebe estimated that 95 percent of the fish he caught down to thirteen thousand feet in Bermuda waters could produce light. It also occurs in sea animals that exist in other kinds of darkness; a marine "earthworm" found among piles of decaying sea grasses along the Gulf of Mexico coast produces a luminous "spit."

But many sea creatures of the shallows also bioluminesce, for largely unknown reasons. When I swam in Long Island Sound, two very different kinds of animals lit up— each a kind of firefly of the sea. One was a dinoflagellate, the tiny *Noctiluca* (the Latin name means "night light"), which occurred in huge numbers—they were like blue sparkles drifting through the blackness. The *Noctiluca* generates "cold fire," dissipating only 1 percent of its energy as heat as compared with 90 percent in a conventional flame. The others were ctenophores, also known as comb jellies, globular jellyfishlike blobs of one to four inches with distinctly lit longitudinal blue lines that form interesting patterns throughout their bodies. Ctenophores are made up almost completely of water and a small amount of salt; only about 1 percent of them is animal protein.

Both categories of animals occasionally flash on their own, but agitate them by pushing through the water and they mark your every movement. Tom Horton in *An Island Out of Time* wrote about a *Noctiluca* bloom so pronounced that even the old-time Chesapeake baymen were wowed. One swore he read his Bible at 3:30 A.M. in the glow of wavelets. Crabbers watched shoals of bluefish streak below like luminous torpedoes. A diver in an enclosed chamber once tried to quantify the abundance of ctenophores in the Patuxent River where it meets the Chesapeake Bay. Over six hours, an average of forty-eight ctenophores per minute passed the window. Extrapolating this to the width of the river, he calculated that 1,218,816,000 ctenophores were carried by in a single tide!

Mariners have long described bioluminescent seas; one record of the descriptive terms used included: *broad belts, ribbons, rivers, milky patches, bars moving at great speed, flashing spots, white water, beams of light, pale blue—horizon to horizon, cloudlike patches,* and *large anticlockwise pinwheels,* among others. These light trails are not at all appreciated by night anglers, though. When casting for striped bass and other species, a fisherman's lures and line glow unnaturally, which usually spooks wary gamefish. One angler described his fly as look-ing like a "dead chicken" and his line like "transatlantic cable." This "fire in the water" is most pronounced on new-moon nights when the bioluminescence is starkly contrasted with the darkness; some anglers choose to fish during bright full-moon periods to minimize the effect.

This quiet and compelling natural show is available around much of North America's coastal waters, especially during summer. Worldwide, the Olympics of biolumines-cence occurs in the Caribbean near the Puerto Rican island of Vieques, where a gallon of water may contain as many as 720,000 glowing dinoflagellates. Puerto Mosquito, its best-known bioluminescent bay, is crammed with a dinoflagel-late named *Pyrodinium,* meaning "whirling fire" in Greek. Night swimmers and boaters report almost magical experi-ences there: "A swim is like floating through stardust"; "Like swimming in silvery bubbles"; and "Watching fish startled by our boat dart away followed by streaks of light is more exciting than any fireworks display I have ever seen." But the peak experience is to visit it on a rainy night. Each raindrop creates a spot of light, causing the entire bay to emit a bluish white glow.

Another strange bioluminescence phenomenon some-times occurs on West Coast shores—sands that emit small, bluish green "sparks" as they're walked on. These beaches glow from dinoflagellates that under certain conditions bloom on the wet sands.

BLACK SKIMMERS
They leave a wake while flying
From Massachusetts to Texas a large, elegant ternlike bird can be seen feeding in a manner unlike any other bird—

and it sometimes accomplishes this while gliding at speeds faster than the wind. The black skimmer's lower bill is about one-third longer than its upper bill, and as it flies over the waves—often in broad circles—the lower bill cuts the surface, leaving a small wake (hence another of its names—the *cutwater*). When the bird hits an object with its beak, its upper jaw snaps down and grabs hold. If it's a fish, the bird feeds; if the object is a stick or other form of debris, it lets it go. But many skimmers have chips missing from their bills, probably from encountering hard, resistant objects.

Both the extended lower beak and movable upper one are special adaptations that allow the black skimmer to make its living in this unique fashion. Also, because it flies so close to the water, its wing strokes never break the bird's horizontal plane. The chief naturalist for the American Littoral Society and longtime skimmer-watcher Dave Grant proposed an interesting theory to explain why gliding skimmers sometimes travel faster than the wind or coast into a breeze at an angle—that they are aerial sailboats. Grant measured key features of the bird and found that its bill-to-wing ratio approaches that of a sailboat's keel-to-sail area. By adjusting the position of its wings (like the trim of sails), and by immersing its lower bill in the water to act like a centerboard, the skimmer may be able to tack into the wind like a ketch—creating a unique hybrid of aircraft and boat.

The experience of watching black skimmers skimming is made even stranger if they sound off—their call resembles a dog barking. Skimmers tend to chatter constantly as they hunt, perhaps to alert other skimmers to their location as they execute their elegant turns and glissades.

BLAZING BEACH
Not a place to go barefoot

At Pepperell Cove in Maine vacationers were treated to an amazing sight on a late-summer day in 1905. David Penhallow, a botany professor, gave the following account:

> . . . *on the evening of Friday, September 1, the guests at the Hotel Parkfield were startled by the appearance of flames rising from the beach and from the surface of the water, an event of so remarkable and unusual a character as to excite great curiosity and some alarm. The conflagration occurred between seven and eight o'clock in the evening and lasted upwards for forty-five minutes. The flames were about one foot in height. They were accompanied by a loud and continuous crackling noise which could be distinctly heard one hundred yards away, while at the same time there was a very strong liberation of sulphorous acid fumes which penetrated the hotel.*

The beach blazed again across a smaller area on October 4. Professor Penhallow surmised that the source of flammable material was methane and hydrogen sulfide gas given off by decaying plant matter from a salt marsh that had been overlain by a sand beach. He also linked the first blaze to an earthquake that had occurred two days before and may have liberated the gas pocket. Penhallow attributed the first episode to trapped gases because, as he wrote, "When some of the sand was taken into the hotel and stirred in water, bubbles of gas were liberated and produced flame as they broke the surface in contact with the air."

Smoldering shores also occur on the western side of Franklin Bay in Canada's Northwest Territories where the coast is backed for several miles by a steep range known as "Smoking Hills" or "Burning Cliffs." This three-hundred- to five-hundred-foot formation is lined in places by layers of bituminous alum shale; some areas of the cliffs burn for years.

Although flames have not been seen in Maine since the first episodes, divers and shoreline observers have spotted gas bubbles arising in nearby Penobscot Bay, suggesting that a local beach might blaze again.

❧❧❧

BLOWOUT TIDES
The depths laid bare

Most often it's an excess of water that gets people's attention—flooding rivers or the surge that a nor'easter or hurricane can bring. But when winds howl in a direction that blows water away from shore, ebb tides can become extremely low and endanger mariners. Reefs that normally are deep enough to be of no consequence may become serious threats to ship bottoms.

Along the East Coast of North America, the wind that creates blowout tides is the nor'wester. Nor'westers often

follow nor'easters and are associated with cold fronts and high-barometric-pressure systems. A sustained northwest wind at speeds as low as twenty miles per hour may drive water out of bays and estuaries. In April 1975, after almost four days of nor'westers, the low tides were so low in the Chesapeake Bay's Baltimore Harbor that fully loaded ships couldn't embark. These wind-aided tides occur frequently enough in the Chesapeake that a children's book was written about it, titled *Where Did All the Water Go?*

My friend Tom Lakes edits the annual *Hudson River Almanac.* The Hudson River runs from north to south and is well situated for blowout tides from cold nor'westers. One of Tom's entries for early April told of a prolonged northwest wind, during which a gusty snow squall blew so hard he watched a seagull fly backward as it lost ground trying to go forward. These winds exposed great mudflats along the river bottom, a rock reef, old piers, and rarely seen barge skeletons.

If you live on the East Coast and want to see the normally submerged shallows of your local waterway, pay a visit at the celestial low tide under blowout conditions. If the wind happens to coincide with a full or new moon, the effect will be even more dramatic.

∽∾∽

BROWN TIDES
Chocolate waters starve shellfish

Brown tides result from algal blooms, but they don't produce neurotoxins like the red tides (see page 130) of Maine and Canada. Nonetheless, they are a real ecological problem, because they absorb much of the aquatic oxygen, cloud the water, and prevent normal plankton from growing. Noxious brown tides are a recent phenomenon, forming since 1985 at certain mid-Atlantic locations such as Peconic and Great South Bays on Long Island, Barnegat Bay in New Jersey, and Narragansett Bay in Rhode Island.

During a bloom, the tiny *Aureococcus* algae that make up more than 90 percent of the plankton provide a poor food source for larger filter-feeding animals. This causes shellfish to stop growing and reproduction to falter. As a result, brown tides have devastated the important scallop fishery of Peconic Bay and hard clam fishery of Great South Bay. Angling also suffers when brown tides occur.

Major research funding has yet to show why brown tides happen; theories involve overfertilization and reduced freshwater runoff.

∽∾∽

CLAM DIGGER'S ITCH
What happens when you are mistaken for a duck

Also known as swimmer's itch, this unpleasant parasitic infection occurs when humans become involved in the complex life cycle of a tiny trematode worm. The microscopic larvae of the trematode are hosted by periwinkles and mud snails. When the maturing young move on from the snails toward their next hosts, they seek shadows near the surface of the water, which are usually the undersides of water-fowl—but a clam digger or swimmer will suffice.

The result is clam digger's itch or swimmer's itch—a fiercely itching, oozing pustule that resembles a mosquito bite. Each embedded worm causes one pustule, as the human body's defensive system rushes to eliminate the foreign protein; the parasite dies in the skin, producing an infection. The itching usually lasts for a couple of days, but the spot may linger for months. There are no lasting effects—at least not for the human—but the worm's life cycle is short-circuited when it picks the wrong host.

ᔕᕽᔕ

CLAM STRANDINGS

The surf goes clickity-clack

In January 1992 great waves rolled into the New Jersey shore from a coastal storm. These rollers ripped out acres of surf clams from their seabed lairs, carrying them shoreward and flinging them on the beach. Afterward, countless numbers of clams formed swaths along the sandy strand up to two hundred feet wide.

This phenomenon followed similar events that occurred over the same area in 1984 and 1979, but clam stranding has taken place in many other areas, including Rhode Island and Maryland. In the 1979 event windrows accumulated more than a foot and a half deep; one observer estimated that more than 180 million clams were beached. After a few days, the larger piles of meat steamed in the cold March air as they decayed.

Clam strandings, though usually fatal to the clams, can be a mixed blessing for humans. If reached quickly in cool weather and in clean water where regulations allow, they can supply unlimited quantities of clam chowder. Stranded clams were more appreciated as a food source in earlier times. When a violent storm pounded northern New Jersey in January 1884, clams were swept ashore in such great numbers that hundreds of wagon loads were carried off.

Still, freshly stranded, apparently inoffensive clams are not as benign as they seem. After one stranding at a Sandy Hook beach, an angler noticed four sanderlings that were able to fly, but appeared crippled. The birds had stepped into open clams, which closed like steel traps around their ankles.

In a stranding, the clams begin to perish as they open. The surf makes an awesome racket as the shells bang together and dislodge clam meats, which in turn form a natural chum slick. This attracts fish, most often striped bass. Fishermen say conditions are right when the wash has the faint odor of rotting clam juice, and their choice of bait at this time is obvious.

But faint rotting smells can become roaring stenches. When this occurs, some beach communities send in front-end loaders to haul huge loads of clams away to an inglorious end at dump sites.

CLIFFS AND ROCK FORMATIONS

Ocean wrestles with shore—and the product is magnificent

Stand by a rocky wave-battered shore and you'll hear a continual dull knocking and clanging of stone on stone. The breaking waves on a bedrock coast dislodge rock chunks; these stones then become chisels and hammers to further erode the rock base. The energy of twelve-foot breakers has been estimated at 1,755 pounds of pressure per square foot; those of twenty-footers at more than 6,000 pounds per square foot.

In *The Winter Beach,* Charlton Ogburn gave a unique account of these forces by someone who visited a mine under the edge of the sea:

> *When standing beneath the base of the cliff, and in that part of the mine where but nine feet of rock stood between us and the ocean, the heavy roll of the larger boulders, the ceaseless grinding of the pebbles, the fierce thundering of the billows, with the cracking and coiling as they rebounded, placed a tempest in its most appalling form too vividly before me to be ever forgotten. More than once doubting the protection of our rocky shield we retreated in affright; and it was only after repeated trials that we had confidence to pursue our investigation.*

And so the rocky coast is configured, together with the forces of glaciers and currents.

But the sea also has remarkably subtle means of shaping the margins of the coast. Salt-spray fretting occurs high on rock faces where the stone is subjected to infrequent but periodic wetting, and exposed to sunlight. The water penetrates between rock granules and leaves salt crystals behind when it dries, which expand as the rock warms in the sun—slowly chewing away its surface.

Rocky shores almost always display a picturesque ruggedness; nowhere is this more evident than along Canada's east coast, where there are many noteworthy bedrock features. Newfoundland's Gros Morne National Park is named for the province's highest mountain, which rises to 2,633 feet above the sea. On the north side of the Gulf of St. Lawrence, Quebec has the Saguenay Gorge, a fjord with sheer walls that drop more than a thousand feet beneath sea level.

Striking columnar structures can be seen in Maritime Canada. Sea stacks are chimneys of rock separated by erosion from the parent cliff; "flower pots" are flat-topped sea stacks, sometimes reddish brown in color like clay flower pots, that have "flowers" on top in the form of trees and bushes. Sea stacks and flower pots are found at Mingan Archipelago National Park Reserve near Havre-St.-Pierre, on the north shore of the Gulf of St. Lawrence, Quebec (across from Anticosti Island). Percé Rock, a limestone massif with a natural arch, can be seen on the gulf's opposite shore at Percé on Quebec's Gaspé Peninsula. A second arch existed slightly seaward until 1845, when it succumbed to erosion. Near Lunenburg, Nova Scotia, are the Ovens, a series of deep caverns gouged out of the rocky cliffs by waves.

The Bay of Fundy and Gulf of Maine region offer a wealth of seaside structures. The Rocks Provincial Park in New Brunswick near Moncton features red sandstone flower pots. Whirlpools and noisy "thunderholes"—cliffside pockets where waves appear to explode—are found at Moosehorn National Wildlife Refuge in Lubec near the mouth of the Bay of Fundy. Canada's Grand Manan Island, just offshore from Maine's Campobello Island, has four-hundred-foot cliffs— the highest on the Atlantic coast south of Newfoundland. At the foot of these cliffs are boulder beaches with the desolate charm of Alaska. Grand Manan also has an impressive wave-carved stone arch called "Hole in the Wall."

Not far to the south in the United States, Maine's Machias Bay islands are a world of caves and arches. Cadillac Mountain on Mount Desert Island in Acadia National

Park is the highest point on the eastern seaboard north of Rio de Janeiro. The 1,530-foot Cadillac Mountain can be scaled by road. The mountain has a huge boulder anomalously perched on it—a "glacial erratic" swept there by ice from far inland. Mount Desert Island also has a deep, five-mile-long gash through bedrock shoulders 852 and 681 feet tall that has been widely considered the U.S. East Coast's only fjord (although the Hudson River sometimes gets honorable mention). But Somes Sound, as impressive as it may be, lacks certain characteristics of a true fjord such as a mound of glacial sediment at its mouth. Thus, instead of a fjord it may be a *fjard,* a Scandinavian term for a less grand, but still glacially carved embayment drowned by the sea.

Mount Desert Island's Thunder Hole is a cave at the end of a fifty-foot-long canyon in the granite, floored beneath the sea surface. Surging down this corridor, a wave slaps against the air in the dome of the cave in the manner of a drumhead. Ogburn described the thunderhole phenomenon: "As the wave recoils the water in the passageway sways sullenly for a bit like some monster which has ineffectually assaulted an obstruction and stands shifting its weight and glowering about it. Then suddenly, with an effect of as if the water was gathering itself together, another wave hurtles into the cave, and once more there is a deep reverberating *boom*." Fortunately, you can view it from behind the safety of a railing. At nearby Anemone Cave the sea has bored a hole eighty-two feet into the rock and formed a cavern that glistens with sea anemones, rockweed, and coralline algae. And the island's Otter Cliffs offer examples of sea stacks.

In *Islands in Time,* Philip Conkling wrote of a Maine island with a most unusual cave—one that is accessible only at low tide under calm conditions, but that stretches clear across the isle. It's definitely not a place to linger as the tide rises. (A similar formation occurs at Battle Rock State Park near Port Orford, Oregon.) Monhegan Island, Maine, has steep seaward-facing cliffs that are exposed to the full force of storms; spray may cover the spruce at one cliff known as White Head a hundred feet above the sea.

On Cape Cod's outer beach, the erosion of the faces of the cliffs (up to 175 feet high) above the Great Beach occurs at the rate of 3 to 4 feet per year. Behind the cliff crown, the land slopes downward, an indication that these glacial hills were at one time much higher and are now more than half eroded away. South of Cape Cod and along Gulf of Mexico shores, coastal heights are primarily sand dunes, which measure in the tens of feet.

On the Pacific coast there are eight volcanic peaks between Morro Bay and San Luis Obispo, California. The tallest of these is Morro Rock, a 576-foot-high dome, fifty acres wide at its base, that juts incongruously out of the surrounding estuarine and sand spit flatness. Farther north, Monterey Bay has windswept cedars clinging to eight-hundred-foot-high cliffs; the escarpment climbs to as high as eleven hundred feet at Big Sur State Park. The steep sandstone cliffs at San Gregorio State Beach Park are known for trapping and reflecting the considerable sound of the surf, resulting in a deep-throated, one-noted ongoing roar that lingers in the memory when you leave to join the suddenly overly quiet rest of the world. Natural rock bridges can be seen at Anacapa Island and, of course, at Natural Bridges State Beach, in Santa Cruz County, California. Mendocino County's coast is characterized by towering sea stacks adjacent to rocky promontories that thrust into the ocean.

Whalehead Island at Whalehead Beach, Oregon, is a massif that not only is shaped like a whale's head but also features a spouting horn, causing spray to shoot up from the island's "head" when the tide is right. Oregon's Cape Perpetua has 700-foot cliffs, while Cape Sebastian sports the seaward side of a sheer mountain that tops out at 1,722 feet. Near Cape Perpetua is the Devil's Churn, a lava chasm that funnels waves to photogenic crashes. This seething chasm is actually a collapsed sea cave; its wild waters have a tendency to generate sea foam, which can sometimes be seen in fluffy chunks flying upward of a hundred feet with the wind. Not far away is an undersea cave called Cooks Chasm, which spouts spray at high tide. Near Florence is the commercially run Sea Lion Caves, the world's largest sea cave, which extends a thousand feet into a headland. Wave action there excavated layers of soft volcanic ash to cut the cave through its hard basalt surroundings. Visitors descend a hundred feet by elevator through solid rock.

British Columbia boasts the famed Malaspina Galleries—not an art museum, but a sandstone sea cave with a wide ledge that looks like a petrified wave cresting overhead. The same province's Graham Island has a huge glacial erratic boulder by the sea that tiptoes on a tiny stone base. It is named, of course, Balance Rock. Agate Beach at Naikoon Provincial Park has a great rock formation called Tow Hill— a huge basalt outcropping formed by molten lava that welled up through cracks in the earth's crust, followed by a glacier that scoured bedrock on the seaward side, leaving the classic inclined structure the French call a *roche moutonnée*, meaning "boulder mountain." At the base of Tow Hill there is a thunderhole known as the Blow Hole where water explodes skyward at midtide.

Watching winter storms strike rocky shores is becoming popular on the Pacific coast. Shore Acres State Park in Oregon has a glass-walled observation building overlooking high cliffs where visitors can watch the onslaught of storm waves. And a Vancouver Island inn has even miked the establishment so that guests can hear the pounding surf from the inside.

~~~

COASTAL FOGS
Looking through pea soup

There are few situations as disorienting to mariners as being enveloped in fog. Sound carries strangely and perceptions of direction go askew, sometimes fully reversed. Wyman Richardson called it the terror of all navigators—after being caught in a fog while canoeing in the Nauset Marsh, he wrote:

> *And then, silently and relentlessly, small puffets of fog come drifting across the dunes "on little cat feet." A slight chill creeps up your spine; the extra sweater is retrieved from under the bow. Old Sol, a moment ago so strong and invincible, suddenly begins to lose his power. A cold air from the east riffles the water. And then, all at once, your world is blotted out.*

Only a compass can help.

Although fogs can occur anywhere across North America that conditions allow, nowhere are they as common or pronounced as along the seacoast, where they sometimes come "pea soup" thick. Coastal fog is slightly brackish to the taste. The fog is formed from condensation around tiny drops of water that arise from the sea surface. Although broken waves or breaking surf do not throw the droplets high in the air, they are picked up by wind currents and carried into the atmosphere.

Fog often forms where there is a large temperature difference between air masses, such as above where warm- and coldwater currents meet. Generally, when the air is warmer than the water, fog is possible. But it also erupts where cool air flows over warm water, even in winter when the icy atmosphere sits above seas that, although cool, may be tens of degrees warmer—sparking the "steam" that is a bane to mariners.

In colonial days, captains steering sailing vessels along rocky New England shores in the "thick-o-fog" listened for the "rote"—the rumbling noise of the sea upon rocky shores, which helped orient them. This seventeenth-century British term is now obsolete in England, but it has survived in New England (and perhaps elsewhere if we "learn by rote").

Fog can be predicted easily by knowing the actual temperature and the dewpoint—the temperature at which the air, as it cools, can no longer hold all of its humidity as a gas. If in evening this "dewpoint spread" begins to narrow, fog can occur. A zero- to ten-degree spread portends fog before midnight, and slow to clear. A ten- to twenty-degree gap suggests fog between midnight and dawn, clearing in late morning. A discrepancy of twenty to thirty degrees can generate a fog just before sunrise, clearing quickly.

Fog is unpredictable in its wanderings and persistence. It may sit offshore as a dark, ominous bank. It is common on outer Cape Cod, where although it doesn't always reach land, it forms about one out of every three days and where even a slight shift of wind can envelop the seaside in a dank soaking mist. Another shift and the sun may break through, the fog simply dissipating in minutes, or tearing apart gradually in streamers. Fog is rare over the Chesapeake Bay's temperate waters, but it's frequent along the cooler ocean coast not far away at Delaware's Cape Henlopen. In *The In-*

land Sea, Morton Hunt, recognizing the difficulty mariners have in predicting when a fog may lift, provided a foolproof formula. Simply look up at the sky and with conviction announce that the fog will burn off inside an hour. The time estimate is usually incorrect, but the prediction is eventually justified if made often enough.

Maine's famous fog influenced its settlement patterns. The coast of Maine has hundreds of islands, many of which were inhabited by European colonists. But typically the northern ends of the islands were settled earlier and more densely than their southern shores. The determining factor seems to have been the chilling effect on the islands' southern ends of coastal fogs that roll in from the Gulf of Maine and set back farmer's crops.

Santa Barbara, California, known for its Mediterranean climate, is dangerous for ships, partly because of its fog. A dense cloud habitually hangs offshore, and prevailing winds blow furiously through the funnel between the mainland and the channel islands. Because of these conditions and yet minus a major harbor, Santa Barbara has gained a reputation as a West Coast graveyard for ships second only to the Columbia River bar and the Golden Gate region.

The Golden Gate and San Francisco as a whole receive rolling fog banks off the ocean almost every day between June and September. This fog is responsible for the average summer high temperature of sixty-four degrees, as well as for Mark Twain's famous quote that "the coldest winter I ever spent was summer in San Francisco." Not far to the north, Point Reyes has the foggiest (and windiest) federal weather station between Mexico and Canada. And northern California's "Lost Coast" is said to have only two seasons: six months of rain and six months of fog.

∽∾∾

CORAL REEFS

Undersea gardens

Coral reefs are the fantasy landscapes of the sea world. Towers, mounds, and fans of hard and soft calcium carbonate form undersea gardens in a broad palette of colors. And healthy coral reefs provide homes for a vast community of other organisms as true exemplars of biodiversity.

But many of the world's reefs are suffering. In some places impoverished fishermen spread cyanide over the corals to quickly poison and harvest reef fishes; the toxicant kills the microorganisms that build the reefs, too. And in locations where other kinds of overfishing have upset delicate ecological balances, smothering algal slimes and coral-eating and burrowing invertebrates such as urchins and starfish are causing declines.

In the mostly temperate United States, the tropical and subtropical coral reefs have a limited distribution. Because they require temperatures above sixty-four degrees, they are restricted to southern Florida and the Florida Keys. Less well-developed coral heads or outcrops of coral are also found along the west coast of Florida to the panhandle and at a few locations off the Texas coast.

Coral reefs are easily explored by snorkeling. Simply drifting overhead allows you to view a kaleidoscopic array of shapes and colors, including sea fans, starlet and brain corals, fire corals, and, rising above them, staghorn and elkhorn corals. Interspersed are large numbers of small, bright fish of multitudinous species—and, if you're lucky, a few more impressive animals such as a moray eel, barracuda, grouper, octopus, or squid. Although the West Coast's chilly waters lack coral reefs, they do have lush kelp beds that provide snorkelers with a similarly rich, garden-like experience.

A very accessible and popular location with twenty miles of fringing reef is the John Pennekamp Coral Reef State Park at Key Largo. Biscayne Bay near Miami also offers fine coral reefs. Although some kinds such as fire corals cause pain if touched, it's important to remember that many corals are fragile and may wither if handled.

∾∾

CROCS AND GATORS
Like sharks with feet

America's great coastal and river reptiles—crocodiles and alligators—are little changed in two hundred million years. Both are sharklike in that they are large, evolutionarily primitive, potentially dangerous, and not intellectually endowed—they can exceed five yards in length, but their brains make up less than 1 percent of their body mass.

The American crocodile is now a rare beast—the least common reptile in North America. Once found widely across northern South America, Central America, Mexico, many Caribbean islands, and the south tip of Florida, the crocodile exists mainly in scattered relict populations. In Florida its numbers fell to as few as two hundred in 1978, three years after it was declared an endangered species. Today it has risen to perhaps five hundred individuals, with hopes of returning it to its original estimated abundance of two to three thousand.

The crocodile is mainly a creature of saltwater and brackish habitats, especially mangrove-lined estuaries, although some live in fresh waters well inland in locations in other countries, and even in a landlocked highly saline lake 125 feet below sea level in the Dominican Republic. In Florida a few have been found living and breeding in the discharge canals of a nuclear power plant—kind of a croc Shangri-la with its steady warm water and its being off limits to humans. And spotting one offshore is not out of the question. Although the crocodile is a backwaters kind of creature, it has been found far out at sea and has traveled hundreds of miles across the ocean to reach isolated volcanic islands.

Recently scientists located more than fifty crocodile nests on Key Largo, Florida Bay, and Biscayne Bay near Miami, in a range that is slowly expanding up both sides of the Florida peninsula. Adults have been found as far north as Fort Lauderdale on the east shore and Sanibel Island on the west.

Crocodiles are lighter in color than alligators and have a narrower snout and more obvious teeth that give them a meaner look than their relatives. They also can swim swiftly, reaching twenty miles per hour in the water. But it's the alligators that are truly dangerous. In Florida only one crocodile attack on a human has been documented, and that occurred in 1925, when a fourteen-footer seized a surveyor in Biscayne Bay after he'd fired two gunshots at the animal. The surveyor died, but the crocodile survived and was shipped to a Florida tourist trap to perform under the name Zulu.

In contrast, since 1948, there have been seven deaths in more than 220 documented alligator attacks on people in Florida. But alligators are also much more numerous. The primeval Everglades alone is believed to have once held hundreds of thousands of alligators, and possibly as many as one million. Because of draining of the marshes and hunting of them for their hides, however, the population dwindled to about ten thousand by 1970. Today there may be one million once more.

Jack Rudloe in *The Wilderness Coast* noted that the alligator has become tame in the public's collective mind because of its use as a symbol of Florida tourism, as a cartoon character, and as the mascot of sports teams. But he urged respect for what he considers to be a true sea serpent and one of the last authentic monsters on earth. Rudloe himself had a gripping encounter with one that bore down on, rose over, and then seized his unsuspecting terrier at a swimming hole. Rudloe wrestled with the reptile, trying to turn it toward shore. He pounded it, squeezed its throat, and pulled on its jaws, but the beast's strength and instinct to secure its prey were unstoppable. The gator carried Rudloe deep into the blackwater depths before he let go to save himself.

Rudloe also told the story of an attack on a human. Over the objections of lifeguards at Wakulla Springs, a young man swam away from the cordoned-off bathing area and snorkeled downriver to a spot where dozens of large alligators lay sunning. "An hour later tourists aboard the jungle-cruise boats spotted an enormous 'gator dragging something through the water, and then saw the grisly sight of the young man's head and torso lifted up in its jaws."

The alligator tolerates lower temperatures than the crocodile, allowing it a greater range in North America—from south Texas to North Carolina. If you're really lucky, you might see a crocodile and an alligator together in the wild. Once on a visit to Flamingo, the little community at the south end of Everglades National Park, I saw several alligators lazing about the main canal right where it flows into Florida Bay. Then I noticed that one of them was much lighter colored, with a different-shaped snout—an American crocodile communing with its cousins.

DOLPHIN BOW RIDING
The sea's brightest and most playful

One of the most intelligent animals on earth is also among the most playful. Pliny the Elder wrote of the dolphin: "It does not dread man, as though a stranger to him, but comes to meet ships, leaps and bounds to and fro, vies with them in swiftness, and passes them even when in full sail."

Dolphins have many beguiling behaviors, including flipper slapping, breaching, spinning, spyhopping (raising high out of the water and rotating to scan the surroundings), and, of course, porpoising. But chief among them is bow riding in front of large moving vessels. Powerboats, as they press through the water, create pressure waves in front of their bows strong enough to propel dolphins with little effort—kind of like updrafts carrying hawks. And it may be

anthropomorphizing, but many witnesses can't help believing that the dolphins bow ride for the sheer joy of it.

Bottle-nosed dolphins are particularly famous for bow riding, but all kinds may do it. An Australian fisherman once saw spotted dolphins riding in the bow wave of his boat, but they gave way to a group of common dolphins, which yielded to a pod of bottle-nosed dolphins. It wasn't clear if this was a hierarchy or simply taking turns, but regardless, the mariner was entertained.

A colleague of mine once saw a remarkable combination of two marine phenomena. While sailing a boat off the northeast coast of Florida, he and his shipmates were treated to the spectacle of a herd of about a dozen dolphins streaming around their vessel on a night with strongly bioluminescent waters. The animals bow rode, swam alongside, and crossed the boat's wake repeatedly, as supple, glowing forms. He especially enjoyed how they would momentarily "black out" when they leapt and "light up" again when they reentered the sea.

DUST OR SAND DEVILS

Hang on to your reading material

Dust devils are little whirlwinds that form in fair weather over land. But they also happen over sandy beaches, where they are called sand devils.

I witnessed a sand devil one hot afternoon on a crowded New York City beach. From about a hundred yards away I heard loud exclamations as the people in the area where the sand devil was developing began to react to the strange event. Everyone else who sensed this happening stood and watched as frightened individuals near the devil ran while beach umbrellas, paper, and towels spiraled upward. But the little tempest soon fizzled, possessions were gathered, and beach life returned to normal.

Australians have put more creative effort into naming the sand devil, calling it a "Willy Willy" or "Cockeyed Bob."

ᔂᔂᔂ

EEL ELVER MIGRATIONS
Great but cryptic invasions

In a chapter on eels in her book on nature spectacles in New Jersey, Joanna Burger wrote, "By the light of the moon, a million glassy threads with beady eyes swim frantically up the narrow stream, against the current, bound for water they have never known." But this describes only the most observable phase in an eel's long existence. Eels have one of the most unique life cycles among fish—kind of the reverse of the chinook and other Pacific salmon, which travel the ocean but spawn in rivers and then die.

For centuries, no one knew where eels came from. Because they were never found with ripe roe, it was believed they came into existence in spontaneous fashion. Aristotle declared that eels arose from the mud; others held that they sprang from small worms or horse hairs that fell on water. It wasn't until 1925 that the mystery was solved. A Danish marine biologist, Johannes Schmidt, traveled thousands of miles across the North Atlantic, capturing eel larvae in fine-meshed nets. By plotting the distribution of the smaller specimens, he zeroed in on a broad spawning area in the Sargasso Sea, south of Bermuda.

In these ultraclear, quiescent waters, adult eels spawn and die. Their eggs float, drifting, and then hatch into larvae that are carried for about a year by currents toward North America. These flattened, transparent "glass" eels metamorphose into narrow, roundish, grayish black "elvers" as they ascend freshwater systems, from the largest rivers to mere trickles. They then spend from about twelve to twenty years growing and maturing, until they turn silver and their eyes enlarge preparatory to the long migration to the Sargasso Sea to complete the cycle.

Glass eels are so transparent that newsprint may be read through them. But despite their ethereal nature and tiny size, they have been fished heavily in recent decades because of the strong Japanese market. In Japan glass eels are stocked in ponds to be grown to adults for seafood. U.S. fishermen were receiving three hundred dollars per pound for live glass eels, and growers were paying twenty-five hundred dollars per pound at the other end. The strain on the eel population is obvious when you realize that it takes two thousand glass eels to make a pound.

In the 1990s glass eel fisheries grew up fast and became ugly as harvesters fought over good sites. New regulations ensued, restricting harvest, but the rewards were too tempting to obey these laws—poachers even "gave up" a colleague to be purposefully caught to distract conservation officers while they continued to fish and make fortunes. The growing harm to the resource, however, caused most states to close these fisheries entirely.

Burger recommended Cheesequake Park in New Jersey, only thirty miles from Manhattan, for viewing the glass eel migration. The most reliable period there is late February through April, and night is better than daytime; farther north the runs may occur into May. A little investigation of small clear streams, particularly at low tide and at spillways where glass eels concentrate, from the Gulf of Mexico to the Canadian Maritimes, should reveal many more instances of this phenomenon.

ᔕᔕᔕ

ELECTRIC FISH
An odd defense

For anyone who's been told never to throw water on an electrical fire, the idea that there are fish in the sea that defend themselves with self-generated shocks is difficult to believe. But a well-timed discharge can freeze the jaws of an oncoming predator or jolt prey into easy submission.

The famous and highly charged electric eel can stun a horse, but it is strictly a South American animal. Still, North America is host to a number of electric fish, mostly rays. A ray's electric organs are derived from striated muscle fibers. In other animals these muscles produce only weak electric charges associated with movement. But in rays they are modified as stacks of flattened cells that constitute about one-sixth of the individual's total weight and are situated on its bottom surface. Primary electric organs on each side of the head are defensive; secondary organs behind are much weaker and may exist for communication. Like a battery, a ray's closely spaced discharges become progressively weaker, until finally exhausted.

The voltage range of electric rays is broad, from 8 to 220 volts among species. The West Coast's lesser electric ray has been found to emit discharges up to thirty-seven volts. Torpedo rays reach one hundred volts—and possibly double that—but these dangerous animals are limited mainly to sandbars offshore from river mouths. Contact with a large ray may result in a shock strong enough to knock over and temporarily disable a person; the sensation has been likened to being hit by a very large fist. But recovery is usually uneventful. A Pacific torpedo ray uses its electrical powers to great advantage—at night it rises into the mid-depths to shock mackerel, wrapping its wings around the stunned fish and gulping them down headfirst.

An electric fish unrelated to rays is the stargazer, with two species found from New York to the Gulf of Mexico. Stargazers get their name from eyes situated on top of their heads that look upward; this arrangement serves them in finding prey as they lie buried in the sand. Modified muscles behind the eyes can provide a shock strong enough for anglers to want to avoid.

Electric rays were used cleverly by ancient Romans for medicinal purposes. They believed that chronic painful headaches could be relieved forever by placing a live black torpedo ray on the afflicted area. They also treated gout by placing a torpedo ray under wet feet until the legs were numb to the knee. Aspirin may be considered an advance beyond this.

∞∞∞

FALCONS
Coastal blurs

Peregrine falcons are the fastest birds in the world; on a power dive or "stoop" they can reach speeds of two hundred miles per hour. They are widespread, being found on all continents except Antarctica, but nowhere are they numerous. The bird's imperious qualities—fierceness, beauty, dazzling speed, and grace—fuel the imagination; ancient Egyptians believed the falcon was a cosmic deity whose body represented the heavens and whose eyes symbolized the sun and the moon.

Peregrine populations in the East crashed by the mid-1960s because of DDT contamination, which so thinned their eggshells that they broke during incubation. In 1965

there were none left in the eastern United States. But after DDT use was banned, largely because of the awareness that stemmed from Rachel Carson's classic writing on the subject, *Silent Spring*, levels of the pesticide in the environment waned. The salt marshes around New Jersey's Barnegat Bay were selected for the first introductions of captive-bred falcons, and they took hold there, nesting by 1980.

Peregrines are not strictly a seaside species, but they are often found along the coasts. They have recently reestablished themselves around New York City, with fourteen pairs nesting on the Big Apple's bridges. They can sometimes be seen along beaches near the mouth of New York Harbor making attacks on sanderlings and other shorebirds. Wyman Richardson observed that on Cape Cod, they often pursue red-backed sandpipers.

Peregrines form part of the annual migration of hawks and other raptors that can be viewed at strategic sites along the East Coast. Good viewing locations include the cliffs at Gay Head on the island of Martha's Vineyard, and on Block Island. On the West Coast there is a much-beloved colony of peregrines on California's Morro Rock at Morro Bay.

Peregrines winter at the Chesapeake Bay Bridge near Annapolis, Maryland, but not for the local seabird prey; instead, they feast on the hordes of pigeons that dwell beneath it.

∽∾∽

FIDDLER CRAB DROVING AND GHOST CRAB WANDERING

The army that retreats sideways

Sometimes in a muddy drain of a marsh you can hear the sharp crackling sound of the moving "shell armor" of a fiddler crab army before you sight them. At Chokoloskee Island near Everglades City, they retreat over sand flats into the mangroves by the thousands when a human approaches. But when fiddler crabs move about in sizable hordes on their own, it's called droving, a behavior that still lacks a good scientific explanation.

Fiddler crabs have some unique features, including that they always travel sideways, and that males have one greatly enlarged claw—their fiddle—usually on their right side. These oversized appendages are useless for feeding with, but

come breeding season they form excellent weapons for jousting with other males and for waving around to attract females—a form of sexual selection in which the larger the claw, the more desirable the claw owner.

Fiddler crabs are well adapted to inshore life and tides, having gills to breathe underwater at high tide and a form of lungs to breathe air at low tide. Fiddlers dig burrows, which they linger near while feeding, much like prairie dogs, ready to dart underground if danger appears. (They don't appear to have individual ownership of burrows, however, but simply use any that are available.) Their burrows may be two feet deep; as the tide rises the fiddler retreats to its home, fashioning a sediment plug to trap air below. When the tide recedes, the crab cautiously reemerges. All this burrowing makes fiddler crabs the earthworms of marshes, turning the sediment over and helping to aerate it.

There are three kinds of fiddler crabs on the Atlantic coast. Mud fiddlers and sand fiddlers may occur in the same regions, but the former prefers muddy ditches and banks, whereas the latter favors compact sandy or muddy flats. The red-jointed fiddler is the largest of the three and is found in mildly brackish marshes. Although they are too small to be eaten by humans, fiddler crabs are harvested for bait for crab-eating fish such as tautog and sheepshead.

Some true sea crabs will voluntarily walk on land when their survival dictates. Blue claw crabs are a much-sought-after Atlantic species that flourishes in coastal salt ponds. But if temperatures plunge in autumn and the ponds are not open to the sea, the crabs may cross the sand by the scores or hundreds to avoid freezing in the shallows.

Fiddler crabs have a close relative, the ghost crab, that verges even more closely on the terrestrial. Their pale color lends them their name; as mobile land dwellers they stand unusually high on their legs for a crab, lifting their carapace off the sand. I once visited Folly Beach, South Carolina, and was amazed to see good-sized crabs scurrying across the streets like squirrels do near my New York home. Although once considered a southern species, they've recently expanded their range into central New Jersey. Ghost crabs dig long burrows to depths of a yard or more that may be situated hundreds of feet from the water's edge; they may forage as much as a quarter mile inland, but must wet their gills with salt water several times a day. Although they may emerge from their holes at any time to forage, they are far more active at night. Take a flashlight and don't worry too much about stepping on them—they're probably faster than you are.

FISH "BLITZES"

Pandemonium under the surface, and often above it, too

If you see fishermen running wildly along the shoreline, or boats with anglers charging to a small patch of the sea, chances are they've spotted a "blitz." A blitz, short for the German *blitzkrieg*, or "lightning war," is when a school of gamefish corrals or rushes a school of smaller baitfish.

A blitz is visible to anglers because the water boils with the leaps and splashes of predators and the panicked prey they herd to the surface. Many kinds of gamefish may blitz. In northeastern coastal waters, a surface commotion usually signals striped bass, bluefish, false albacore, or bonito. Sometimes the species are mixed; somewhat lazier stripers may follow the more energetic bluefish and ambush the baitfish flushed by the blues. On the West Coast striped bass or yellowtails may blitz. In more tropical waters, jacks, snook, or tarpon launch feeding frenzies. And blitzes (under other names) occur anywhere in the world where

gamefish school up—when sea bass erupt on the surface in British waters, the locals call it a "munch up."

There is one sure sign of a blitz from a distance: If you spot a dense aggregation of birds hovering over and diving into an area of water, there are feeding gamefish below. Sharp-eyed and always opportunistic seabirds, such as gulls, terns, and gannets, flock to this carnage from far away for the easy pickings it provides. The birds seize either the live, swimming, but highly vulnerable baitfish, or pieces of them bitten and then left behind by the attacking gamefish. Another, more subtle sign of blitzes is a smell in the air that fishermen say resembles cucumber. When predators chop small prey fish, they rupture their stomachs, which often contain partially digested phytoplankton. These algae may impart a garden odor, signaling that a blitz just occurred. The wise angler hangs around—gamefish often regroup and blitz again.

A particularly exciting part of a shoreline blitz is the opportunity to see gamefish in the shallows. In the clear waters of Montauk, New York, I've seen pods of striped bass shadowing the more aggressive bluefish as they savaged anchovy schools. Another time I waded out to a boulder, only to see a group of large stripers sweep through the shallows behind me as they searched for victims.

Sometimes a surfside blitz provides a special visual feast—the sight of gamefish swimming through peaked waves right before they break. When this is viewed through the low-angled rays of dawn or dusk, the effect is spectacular as the predators become silhouetted in the backlight—a primal scene on an aquatic stage.

In a blitz the seabirds usually fly right over the heart of the fish schools as they move along, serving as aerial markers as to where to cast. It's not uncommon for anglers following along to hook or lasso a bird by accident. If this happens, it's best to slowly reel the angry bird in and then to drape a cloth over its head to calm it before untangling it. But resume casting—although blitzes sometimes last for hours, they are often over in just minutes, and there are few more exciting moments to an angler than those experienced while fishing a blitz.

FISH KILLS

Death in droves

There aren't many coastal scenes more depressing than a massive fish kill. Dead bodies litter the surface. If enough time has passed since the die-off, and especially if the weather is warm, the horrid smell of putrefying flesh scents the air. Nearby residents may be alarmed—is there something bad in the water killing the fish? Something they should be worried about?

Not for the most part. Although fish kills stem from many causes and are notoriously indecipherable, these grisly scenes more often occur naturally than from unseen contaminants. Sometimes pathogens—infections or parasites—are the problem. At other times poor environmental conditions lower oxygen levels, suffocating fish in their own medium.

A dramatic kind of fish kill, involving a herringlike fish called menhaden, is frequently seen along the East and Gulf Coasts. The menhaden, often locally called "mossbunker" or "bunker" for short, is a favored food of the bluefish. Often, tightly packed schools of menhaden are herded like cattle by the toothsome and voracious blues. Sometimes the bluefish corner them in coves or dead-end creeks; usually these shallows are warmer and hold less oxygen. As the panicky prey mill about and try to avoid the rushes of the predators, they use up the available oxygen and begin a death spiral; the stress causes the menhaden to evacuate their intestines, further deteriorating surrounding water quality. The attacks, combined with their declining ability to respire, cause cardiovascular failure and the menhaden succumb, swimming feebly and then dying in place. The bluefish swim off satiated, having taken their toll, but the vast majority of menhaden mortalities never suffer a bluefish bite.

The scale of these menhaden die-offs can be massive, numbering in the millions. And for those who assume such devastation must in some way be unnatural, possibly related to pollution, it is important to note that the early Dutch explorer Jasper Danckaerts recorded this phenomenon in the New York region in 1679—well before pollution would have had any effect.

Although fish kills occur for many reasons, the actual cause is often remarkably hard to diagnose. Repeated die-offs in 1997 of longfin smelt in Lake Washington, near Seattle, were examined and analyzed by numerous experts, and many ideas were advanced, including oxygen depletion, supersaturated gases, high temperature, infection, and toxic exposure—yet none of these theories was demonstrated to be correct.

But it is safe to say that oxygen depletion is the most frequent killer. Low oxygen is thought to be responsible for chronic die-offs in the Neuse River in North Carolina and for the all-at-once loss of about twenty million young menhaden in Texas in 1999. In most of these instances, stressful weather conditions exacerbate conditions already degraded by human or animal sewage. Sometimes they spawn algal or dinoflagellate blooms such as "red tides" (see page 130) that quickly diminish oxygen.

Sudden cold snaps also kill fish. A large die-off of striped bass occurred in a Long Island bay after a severe winter chill. Sometimes tropical fish in the shallows of south Florida succumb to sharp cold fronts; hundreds of thousands died in the upper Florida Keys during the winter of 1969–1970.

Probably the most phenomenal coldwater event involved tilefish in the deeps off the mid-Atlantic and New England. This large and commercially valuable species had been discovered only three years earlier south of Nantucket, its existence hidden by its inhabitation of only a narrow band of continental shelf more than sixty fathoms deep that is bathed by a belt of warm water. But in March 1882 vessel after vessel reported traveling miles through multitudes of dead tilefish floating over the entire zone inhabited by it north of Delaware Bay; it was estimated that at least a billion and a half tilefish corpses were spread across some four thousand square miles.

The prevailing theory was that their destruction was caused by a temporary flooding of their habitat by abnormally cold waters. There was fear that the species had been lost—and only three years after it was discovered! Fishing trials by the Fish Commission between 1882 and 1887 did not yield a single tilefish. But eight were caught in 1892, and fifty-three in 1893; eventually a commercial fishery that provided millions of pounds of tilefish per year redeveloped.

FISH LADDERS AND LIFTS
Going against the flow isn't easy

There are places where you can watch large fresh-from-the-salt fish climb upstream. Anadromous fish—those such as salmon that are spawned in fresh water, go to sea, and then return to rivers to themselves spawn—have been blocked by dams in their upstream migrations in many rivers. At all too many dams, there are no facilities to help fish move past, and the anadromous species either spawn below the barriers or perish from those river systems. But as the public and natural resource managers have become more enlightened about the importance of fish passage, more and more facilities have been retrofitted to old dams or incorporated in the construction of new ones.

One way to allow fish past dams is with kind of a fish highway—special "ladders" that allow fish to work their way up a long sloping channel with partitions, moving through the flow of water chamber by chamber. Some ladders have external observation decks where the public can view fish moving up them, and a few have windows where you can observe them sideways and close up. The fish ladder at Easton,

Pennsylvania, allows shad and other species to pass from the Delaware River to the Lehigh River; fish can be seen from above or from an underground viewing room. In Seattle several kinds of salmon and steelhead (migratory rainbow trout) pass up a twenty-one-step fish ladder to Lake Washington. Six lighted windows provide visitors a glimpse at them. An underwater-level window is also available at a salmon and steelhead ladder near Roseburg, Oregon.

But the mother of West Coast fish ladders is at the Bonneville Dam—the first blockage migratory fish meet as they ascend the mighty Columbia River. Flooding of the Columbia River with the construction of massive dams eliminated natural falls, including the dramatically rugged Celilo Falls where salmon gathered before making great leaps to continue upstream and where Native Americans fished for them off rickety scaffolding. Not only was this colorful fishery lost, but the stillwater reservoirs behind the dams confuse young salmon trying to migrate downstream to the ocean. Nonetheless, the fish ladders—with individual steps in one-foot increments that are forty feet wide, sixteen feet long, and six feet deep—work well enough to sustain runs at more than a million fish, albeit with vastly diminished glory.

An even more artificial alternative to fish ladders in helping fish move past dams is to accomplish it with fish lifts—essentially elevators that bring them up to the level of the lake behind the dam. These devices are usually used where dams are too tall or the geometry of the plunge pool below the dam doesn't allow for a long, inclined fish ladder. Fish are lured to a gathering area with engineered currents, the so-called attraction flow, and then some form of movable gate concentrates them into the actual lift bucket. After that, they go for a short ride, which terminates in their being released in a short canal to swim into the reservoir.

Along the canal there is a fish-viewing room with a large window where biologists count the numbers and kinds of fish passing.

The fish lift at the Conowingo Dam on the Susquehanna River, near Conowingo, Maryland, allowed the greatest recovery of an American shad population across its entire range. A series of large dams that were constructed beginning in 1904 choked off one of the most important spawning rivers for anadromous fish. The annual run of American shad, once in the millions of individuals, dwindled to less than two hundred in the early 1970s. But the fish lift at Conowingo Dam, and other fish passage facilities upriver, have brought the run back to more than a hundred thousand. If you visit the dam during its public hours in April and May, you can ascend a staircase in front of the dam and visit the counting chamber, where you may see multitudes of shad, and sometimes striped bass, catfish, carp, and many other possibilities. A similar facility exists at a dam on the Connecticut River in Holyoke, Massachusetts.

Fish ladders and fish lifts have many trade-offs. "There is no such thing, I have been told by men who were in the business of making them, as a good or even adequate fishway," wrote John Hay in *The Run*. Ladders require little attention, allowing fish to move through at will. Many anadromous species, however, including striped bass and sturgeon, refuse to climb fish ladders. Fish lifts will carry along any species that gather in them, but they require labor-intensive operation and are limited in their capacity.

The best solution to fish passage is the removal of dams. Although many dams are essential for their hydroelectric capabilities and for water storage, North America has numerous dams that have little societal value today but remain standing, causing serious ecological harm, simply through inertia.

Anyone who was along the Kennebec River's shores at Augusta, Maine, on July 1, 1999, witnessed a truly significant phenomenon—the breaching of the Edwards Dam. Battling against the hydroelectric industry, conservationists defeated the relicensing of the dam as an electricity generator, setting an important national precedent. As the torrent of water broke through the breach that day, seventeen miles of water were opened to Atlantic salmon, striped bass, sturgeon, and shad for the first time in 164 years. With sentiment growing for the removal of dams wherever possible, there should be more opportunities to see salmon and other anadromous fish leaping reemerged but original barriers as they once did at Celilo Falls.

⁂

FLOATERS' WEEK
Resurrection of the damned

There is an infamous marine phenomenon that involves cadavers. *Floaters' week* is a term known by mariners for that short window of time when each winter's bounty of murder, suicide, and accident victims that have accumulated underwater rise to the surface, in what I called in my book about New York Harbor, *Heartbeats in the Muck*, "a synchronized resurrection of the damned."

The rising of the dead can occur anywhere, but it is particularly noteworthy in urban harbors where the sheer size of the surrounding population tends to produce more sunken bodies. Bacterial activity is retarded in the cold, but as water temperatures reach about fifty degrees, microbial activity hits a higher gear and any submerged bodies begin to bloat and rise to the surface.

Floaters' week is legendary in New York Harbor, an area that generates more than its share of corpses (although some crime killings are fitted with "cement shoes" and remain forever in the deep). Joseph Mitchell wrote about it in his classic, *The Bottom of the Harbor*, quoting a conservation officer:

> *On an ebb tide, there's an eddy in the elbow that picks up anything loose coming downriver, afloat or submerged, and sweeps it into a stretch of backwater on the Brooklyn side. This backwater is called Wallabout Bay on charts; the men on the dredges call it Potter's Field. The eddy sweeps driftwood into the backwater. Also, it sweeps drowned bodies into there. As a rule, people that drown in the harbor in winter stay down until spring. When the water begins to get warm, gas forms in them and that makes them buoyant and rise to the surface. Every year, without fail, on or about the fifteenth of April, bodies start showing up, and more of them show up in Potter's Field than any other place. In a couple of weeks or so, the Harbor Police always find ten to two dozen over there—suicides, bastard babies, old barge captains that lost their balance out on a sleety night attending to tow ropes, now and then some gangster or other.*

If you encounter a floater, it's best to summon professional help. Long ago, my father was fishing at a crowded New York City pier when a body drifted within sight. One fellow showed interest in retrieving it; egged on by his pier mates, he swam out and dragged it ashore, expecting to be a hero in the eyes of the police. Instead he received a severe scolding, with the officers asserting there could have been two dead bodies instead of one.

✌✌✌

FLYING FISH
Aerial acrobats

Once in the Florida Keys I was riding through the shallows in a small boat when "flocks" of silvery bullet-shaped fish erupted nearby and skipped along the surface, gliding for dozens of yards before plunging back. They were flying fish—one of the most unlikely and graceful creatures in the sea.

Flying fish can grow to a foot and a half, with pectoral fins that reach almost to the tip of the tail. Some flying fish are monoplanes, sporting only the broad pectorals. Others are biplanes, having enlarged ventral fins, too. In all flying fish the lower lobe of the tail fin is elongated as a scudding surface to propel the fish forward and to steer it in the air.

Benjamin Franklin, on a voyage from London to Philadelphia in 1726, was fascinated by flying fish. He wrote:

> When they fly it is straight forward, (for they cannot readily turn), a yard or two above the water; and perhaps fifty yards is the furthest before they dip into the water again, for they cannot support themselves in the air any longer than while their wings continue wet. These flying-fish are the common prey of the dolphin (the fish, not the mammal), who is their mortal enemy. When he pursues them, they rise and fly; and he keeps close under them till they drop, and then snaps them up immediately. They generally fly in flocks, four or five, or perhaps a dozen together, and a dolphin is seldom caught without one or more in his belly.

Franklin and the ship's crew caught dolphins on their journey on a lure made by imitating a flying fish by sticking two feathers on either side of a candle.

Although Franklin understood the basics, much about flying fish has been learned since. Before taking off a flying fish swims just below the surface for some distance, then turns upward and spreads its pectoral fins, leaving the water except for the lower lobe of its tail. Vigorously beating its tail back and forth, it taxis across the surface, picking up speed. Finally, it extends its ventral fins and rises into the air. One-hundred- to three-hundred-foot flights are common at heights of four to five feet, but they've been known to fly a thousand feet and more and to reach heights of thirty-six feet. Most flights last for about ten seconds, though one was clocked at forty-two seconds.

Interestingly, about 75 percent of their flights are made into the wind, meaning that they monitor wave direction or sense the effects of wind in some other way. A low-flying pilot watched them and noted that they changed direction when they touched down, typically taking off at about seventy degrees to the right of the first flight.

It's long been speculated as to why flying fish fly. The answer probably is related to the dolphinfish that hunt them relentlessly. Although they can fly at about the same speed that a dolphinfish can swim, gliding through relatively thin air uses far less energy than thrusting through viscous water.

Flying fish have been caught on hook and line, but it's a true specialty sport. Stranger yet, people have "hunted" flying fish with small-gauge shotguns and light loads as if shooting skeet; because they float, they can be collected as food.

FLYING GURNARDS
Flying fish wannabes

The strange sea-robin-like fish on this book's cover is not a great soarer like the true flying fish. It is found along the East Coast of North America from Massachusetts southward, but this small fish—usually less than one foot long—is rarely caught by anglers. Similar species are found in the Indo-Pacific and Mediterranean.

Early describers were so moved by the fish's form that they greatly embellished the facts. Ancient Greeks and Romans likened them to swallows that flew through the air making noises with their great pectoral fins (they can produce a whistling sound as air passes through their gill openings). In the second century B.C. Oppian classified flying gurnards with scorpions and dragons.

Although flying gurnards can't fly, they can leap. They shoot out of the water in small schools, leaning forward and then disappearing as other groups emerge. This dance is most compelling at night in phosphorescent seas—their underwater paths glow, but they "black out" while airborne. In daylight, leaping flying gurnards may be targeted by gulls and frigate birds.

∽∾∿

FOSSIL CLIFFS AND BEACHES
Ancient organisms revealed to professional and amateur paleontologists alike

Coastal cliffs that bear fossils offer a chance to see plants and animals, literally in their graves, that go back millions to hundreds of million years. Over time, waves and winds erode fossils from cliffs, with many washing back to shore where they can be claimed by the careful searcher. Although most seaside fossils are not large, the occasional find can be spectacular. At one cliff a small boy poking with a stick found something interesting. He called for his father and together they unearthed an intact turtle fossil, more than a foot long, its bones mineralized to agate.

Seaside locations where you can find fossils are surprisingly widespread and numerous. Cape St. Mary's in Newfoundland has Cambrian green and black shales that contain the horseshoe crab's cousins, trilobites—invertebrates that dominated the seas more than three hundred million years ago. In parts of Cape Breton, Nova Scotia, as the waves erode cliffs of shale, fossil ferns and reptiles are revealed; some sandstone cliffs there also contain records of ancient life. The fossil-bearing sea cliffs at Arisaig, Nova Scotia, offer the longest unbroken sequence of four-hundred-million-year-old rocks in North America.

Near the head of the Bay of Fundy at Joggins, Nova Scotia, is a world-class paleontological site—the Joggins Fossil Cliffs. The bay's almost fifty-foot tides scour the seventy-five-foot-tall cliffs, constantly revealing new fossils. These cliffs became famous in 1851 when they were visited by two prominent geologists, Charles Lyell and William Dawson. Although Joggins was already known for an abundance of fossilized tree trunks found in their original rooted positions, Lyell and Dawson noticed tiny bones in one of the stumps. This find turned out to be one of the world's earliest reptiles, and the first evidence that land animals had lived during the Carboniferous period or "coal age," more than two hundred million years ago.

If you want to see additional fossilized tree trunks, visit Odiorne Point, in Rye, New Hampshire. There, at very low tides, you can view the lower portions of tree trunks and the whorls of roots from a forest that was submerged when the sea level rose at the end of the last glacial period. Or try the ocean side of Cape Henlopen, Delaware, where on extreme low tides or after a storm has carried sand away, fields of sea-worn stumps of an old cedar forest that was submerged in historical times can be seen. And at the north side of Montauk Point, New York, low tide reveals white cedar stumps, part of a stand that once stood several hundred yards from the water.

Large swaths of the shoreline of the Chesapeake Bay are exceptionally good fossil-hunting locations; the first fossil described from North America, the four-lined fossil snail in 1658, came from this region. The Calvert Cliffs along the Chesapeake Bay's western shore are a well-known source; three formations along thirty miles of these cliffs span much of the Miocene epoch of ten to twenty million years ago. The Calvert Cliff deposits are among the world's richest in whales and porpoises and other marine mammals. They include sperm whale, several kinds of baleen whales, river dolphins, and beaked porpoises, plus seals and manatees. Crocodiles, freshwater and marine turtles, and many kinds of pelagic bird remains have been reported from the cliffs. One pelicanlike bird stood six feet tall and had a wing spread of perhaps twenty feet. Other fossils seen include vertebrae and scales from fish, various land mammals, and about four hundred kinds of mollusks (of which about 11 percent still live today). The shores of the lower Potomac River are rich in fossil oysters, whelks, moon snails, and other mollusks. Farther south in the Virginia portion of the Chesapeake Bay, Chippokes Plantation State Park has a beach with modern shells, mixed with those from two formations that date back eight to nine million and three and a half to five million years ago, respectively.

Honeymoon Island, in Dunedin, Florida, offers a beach with many fossil-containing rocks. Possibilities for imprints are plants, sponges, coral, and shells, including snails and arks. Generally promising locations in Florida are anywhere bedrock-breaking construction work creates spoil piles near the shore.

Although the washed-up bones of recently dead nonfish vertebrates such as chickens (from discarded meals) and seabirds are common on beaches, true vertebrate fossils beyond fish are not often discovered along the shore. But some beaches offer better odds for this than others. Venice, Florida, has proved highly productive, as has the stretch between St. Petersburg and Fort Myers.

On the West Coast marine fossils can be found at Whites Point in the Palos Verdes area of Los Angeles and in the sandstone cliffs at San Gregorio State Beach Park. Fossilized clam, scallop, and snail shells are found on beaches of Lincoln and Tillamook Counties, Oregon, especially Beverley Beach and between Yaquina Head and Cape Fowl Weather. The sandstone cliffs at Cape Arago yield marine fossils, usually a forebear of the chambered nautilus.

Petrified wood is common on beaches of the Pacific Northwest, particularly in Oregon, Washington, and Alaska. Types of wood may include myrtle, ginkgo, and cedar. In 1998 El Niño storms revealed large two- to four-thousand-year-old stumps in Neskowin and Newport, Oregon.

Alaska's Tancook Island has a well-known fossil beach near the Government Wharf. The fossils are old ones—mainly brachiopods and corals dating back some half a billion years. An easy way to view them is to visit the collection displayed at the local general store.

FROSTFISH

The fish come already frozen

Frostfish is a term for the silver hake, a fish that sometimes throws itself on shore. But unlike shore-spawning species such as grunion and capelin, the silver hake's stranding is a mistake; most don't make it back to sea again.

Silver hake range from Newfoundland to South Carolina but are common from New York northward. They are mainly a deep-sea fish, occurring in depths to about eighteen hundred feet. But sometimes great schools of silver hake chase smaller fish in the shallows. Perhaps due to their unfamiliarity with the shore or their crazed pursuit of their prey, many may strand themselves, especially after dark. When this happens on bitter winter nights they can be easily gathered, but they may be no more supple than baseball bats, if time has allowed them to freeze. If you stumble upon them in subfreezing temperatures, call them frostfish.

GANNETS
Avian aerial bombs

In *The Winter Beach*, Charles Ogburn considered gannets sophisticated looking, with a rakish design. "Slim, tapered, with setback wings, the gannet reminds you of a bow and arrow, and like an arrow it dives from on high. . . ." But from a distance airborne gannets dropping from a hundred feet into the water at sixty feet per second to seize fish look like concrete blocks landing. The large, seven-pound birds throw splashes twelve feet high—imagine the fish's surprise! But the gannet's strategy is different from those of other birds that spear or engulf fish from above: Gannets grab their prey on their way *up*.

Gannets aggregate in huge nesting colonies, including in the Gulf of St. Lawrence, Newfoundland, and Labrador; North America hosts six of the world's twenty-two nesting assemblages. Pristine colonies were once awesome in their plentitude. When Cartier rounded Newfoundland into the Gulf of St. Lawrence in 1534, he came to Bird Rock, a stone island rising more than three hundred feet from the sea; an observer declared that "the birds sit there as thick as stones on a paved street." John James Audubon wrote in his journal of 1833 that the Bird Rock cliffs on which the white birds nested appeared "covered with snow to a depth of several feet. . . ." Get closer today and you'll experience a raucous scene filled with bowing, jabbing, and sky-pointing gannets bickering and defending their territory. But an overall peace is maintained by the birds' social mores; they return to the same precise nesting site every year and manage to coexist in close quarters by using a dozen different movements to indicate intended activities to their neighbors.

Many of these northern seabird populations crashed in the late 1800s. Commercial fishermen would raid nesting sites to kill gannets and other seabirds for their operations. Audubon reported on the brutal practice:

The fishermen who kill these birds, to get their flesh for codfish bait, ascend in parties of six or eight, armed with clubs; sometimes, indeed, the party comprises the crews of several vessels. As they reach the top, the birds, alarmed, rise with a noise like thunder, and fly off in such hurried, fearful confusion as to throw each other down, often falling on each other till there is a bank of them many feet high. The men strike them down and kill them until fatigued or satisfied. Five hundred and forty have thus been murdered in one hour by six men. The birds are skinned with little care, and the flesh cut off in chunks; it will keep fresh for about a fortnight.

Today fifty thousand nest on Bonaventure Island near the eastern tip of the Gaspé Peninsula—the largest colony in the world; the second largest "gannetry" is at Cape St. Mary's on Newfoundland's south coast.

More impressive than individuals are masses of gannets feeding as a unit. Wyman Richardson described perfectly their unique maneuvers after watching a flock of about two thousand feeding off Oregon Inlet at Hatteras Beach. "The birds in the forward edge of the flock were all dropping out of the air into a smother of spray; as they reappeared, the flock had passed by, and they joined the rear, soon to reach the lead again. It was a waterfall of gleaming white birds against a background of gentian blue water." I have seen the same phenomenon at Montauk, New York, and would add that although the gannet attack lacks military precision, they perform this bombardment with the cool efficiency of an experienced guerrilla unit. But as aerially masterful as gannets are, they are equally ungainly on land—sometimes they run to take off and collapse on the ground with a thud.

GREAT LEAPING FISH

Admire them, but get out of the way

Suffice it to say there are few greater surprises than when, without warning, a giant fish leaps out of the water nearby. Once in a while it lands in a boat, causing substantial damage and injury and making the curiosities column of newspapers. Many large species are known to make sudden jumps, the causes of which are difficult to decipher.

Theories abound as to why great fish leap (little fish jump too, but it's less noteworthy and can often be explained as efforts to escape predators). Aristotle, more than two thousand years ago, attributed the desire of swordfish (*Xiphias*) to leap from the water to the irritation caused by parasites, stating that "... beneath their fins they have a little worm which is called oestrus, which resembles a scor-

pion, and is the size of a spider; they suffer so much from
this torment that the Xiphias leaps out of the sea as high as
a dolphin, and in this manner frequently falls upon ships."
This may include the remora fish or shark sucker, not a true
parasite but rather a fish that latches on with a suction cup
and hitches a ride, darting off to pick pieces of food from
the swordfish's kills. Bluefin tuna also leap, somewhat ran-
domly when they are chasing schools of prey fish and in a
unidirectional line when they are simply traveling.

The sturgeon is about as unlikely a leaper as there is
among fish—it's a bottom dweller, often living at great
depths. Yet the Atlantic sturgeon frequently erupts through
the surface. A fisherman I met said he routinely sees them
jumping in lower New York Bay as they head up the Hudson
River to spawn. For some time the founder of the Hudson
River Fishermen's Association offered a thousand-dollar re-
ward to anyone who could snap a photograph of a Hudson
River sturgeon in midleap. No one, including me, was able
to accomplish this, but I have heard some mighty splashes
as the fifty- to two-hundred-pound fish reentered the water.

Alas, I later did see a magnificent sturgeon leap, twisting in the air, far inland in Wisconsin's Lake Winnebago.

Fishermen claim sturgeon leap to knock off leeches or to shake free crayfish they ingested that are pinching their intestines. Other theories include the ideas that they are trying to feed on aerial prey or attempting to shake loose recalcitrant eggs. A new scientific theory is that they create loud percussive splashes to communicate their locations to each other in the dark, turbid rivers they typically dwell in.

One reason leaping fish are dangerous is that they may appear so unexpectedly. Recently, a surfer in Florida didn't know what hit him when, after just getting to his feet on the face of a wave, a seventy-five-pound tarpon vaulted into his face, knocking him unconscious, causing a concussion, and cutting him so that he required fifteen stitches to close the wound.

The modest-sized but arrow-shaped needlefish makes long leaps that sometimes hurt or even kill people. These tropical fish have a long, slender body that may reach six feet. They also have two pointed, elongated jaws. Although most of the time they undulate languidly, when excited they can scull rapidly over the surface of the water. Needlefish also are attracted to light at night and may leap in its direction. These fin-propelled lances have punctured the chest, abdomen, arms, legs, and neck of various people. In 1977 a ten-year-old Hawaiian boy was killed when a needlefish jumped over a net and penetrated his brain.

Some unathletic-looking fish make dramatic leaps. The giant ocean sunfish, often weighing hundreds of pounds, sometimes becomes airborne. When it comes down on its broad, flat flank, it sounds like an oversized manhole cover landing. Great, lumbering basking sharks weighing several tons are able to leap completely out of the water. Even the flat, bottom-dwelling rays leave the sea at times. While bird-ing, a friend saw a manta ray leap off Cape May, New Jersey; these rays can reach more than twenty feet wide and three thousand pounds, and if airborne would capture the atten-tion of even the most ardent bird-watcher.

GRUNION RUNS

This fish spawns above the waterline

If it wasn't for its strange spawning rituals, the grunion would be just another small silvery fish, much like a smelt in appearance. But when the grunion are running, literally leaping onto the shore in droves, it's high holiday time on southern California and Baja, Mexico, beaches; the fishing couldn't be easier. Just grab a bucket and flashlight and start gathering; saucepans, hats, and hands also qualify as regulation equipment. At popular grunion-spawning loca-tions, a mania among the gatherers sets in, aided by the subtle narcotic of almost full moons and the greed that short-term gluts of natural offerings instill. Parties are held under the bright night sky, helped along by beach fires— which also serve to cook fresh grunion skewered on the tra-ditional stick.

If their lying on the beach doesn't make harvesting them simple enough, grunion also assist with their sheer predictability of occurrence—no fish is easier to plan for. Grunion spawn at night shortly after high tide, but only during the second, third, and fourth nights following the full moon in March, April, May, and June. Like surfers, pairs of males and females ride the crest of the wave. When the wave flattens on shore, they swim onward, pushing their tails through the succeeding wave. Then when the water reaches its highest point on the beach and starts to recede, the female digs her tail into the sand and the male throws himself across her in an arched position, and they spawn quickly before returning to the sea on the succeeding wave.

Grunion bury their eggs about two inches below the surface of the sand. But by spawning just after high tide, they capitalize on the tendency for the falling tide to deposit sand on the beach, thereby covering their eggs even deeper. The eggs incubate for two weeks in the warm sand and then hatch on the also-very-high new-moon tides.

A grunion run lasts for only a few hours, but thousands of fish may be on the beach at once. Each female may spawn between four to eight times during the season. The famed California grunion beaches include Silver Strand, Pacific, La Jolla Shores, Del Mar, Doheny, and Carpinteria. The Cabrillo Marine Aquarium in San Pedro schedules a bonfire lecture on the beach prior to watching the grunion show—this is a most cooperative fish!

Grunion have a less famous counterpart on the Atlantic coast, capelin, which come ashore with the breakers to spawn at high tide in parts of the Canadian Maritimes. They also are harvested with dip nets and buckets. In Newfoundland the runs occur every June and July. Fishermen watch for signs of the gathering schools: whales and mobs of seabirds dining just offshore. When the capelin hit the beach, they turn the shores spongy with their sticky, reddish spawn, a foot deep in places. Many return to the sea, but the falling tide maroons many others, leaving some spots waist-deep in fish. Seabirds gather in great flocks for the free meals.

People collect the stranded capelin by the bushel, to fry, smoke, or salt, or to fertilize gardens. And in the old days when cod were still abundant, these big fish would roll through the shallows gorging on capelin while fishermen filled their dories with cod simply by gaffing them as they swam by.

❧❧❧

HAWK MIGRATIONS ALONG THE SEASHORE
Soaring on the coastal highway

Few animal migrations are as visible as those of hawks, which are usually seen well overhead. Although there are many excellent inland sites to watch migrating hawks, the real action occurs along the coasts, nowhere as actively as at Cape May, New Jersey.

The peak period for hawk-watching at Cape May on their migration to Florida and points south is mid-September to mid-October. And viewers will not go alone or unserviced; hawk-watching helps support the local economy as birders pour into this mecca. The main observation platform is owned by the New Jersey Audubon Society; alongside it is a board that provides the hawk tallies for the day—counts made by paid observers.

At Cape May the species most often seen are sharp-shinned hawks, American kestrels, and a few Cooper's, all flying relatively low; higher up, it's mainly ospreys. If you're lucky, you may sight a peregrine, although as many as twenty in a day have been spotted. Even though ospreys and hawks are cosmopolitan, nowhere in the world are they seen in higher numbers than at Cape May. The height of the hawk migration coincides with the peak of the songbird migration, their principal prey. Some days more than a thousand hawks pass over Cape May, perhaps fifty thousand or more in a season. Sustained northwest winds tend to increase hawk passage through the Cape May corridor.

Interestingly, not all types or even age classes of hawks use coastal routes such as the one past Cape May. Broad-winged hawks are known only for their inland migrations because these birds need updrafts to soar, and air heats and rises much more effectively over land than water. When broad-winged hawks meet the expanse of Delaware Bay, they must often move inland to find a narrower crossing. And for some reason the percentage of immature hawks at Cape May and along the coastal route is substantially higher than by chance alone.

At coastal New Jersey's other end, Sandy Hook has a prominent, monitored spring hawk migration, with about four to ten thousand birds seen each season. Peak flights occur during late April and early May. Cape Henry, Virginia, and Cape Henlopen, Delaware, also offer spring viewing of hawks.

A worthwhile hawk-sighting location in Connecticut is Lighthouse Point in New Haven where, from September to November, twenty to thirty thousand broad-winged and sharp-shinned hawks, ospreys, northern harriers, American kestrels, merlins, and peregrine falcons are seen. New York's Fire Island has a hawk-watch on the eastern end of Robert Moses State Park.

South of Cape May, the Eastern Neck Wildlife Refuge in the upper Chesapeake Bay is a reliable site. Kiptopeke, at Cape Charles, Virginia, has one of the highest eastern annual hawk counts, but it's always well below the tally at Cape May. The Outer Banks of North Carolina are known for their flights of falcons, although hawks are also sighted. Pea Island National Wildlife Refuge near Nags Head is a popular location. On the West Coast a substantial hawk flight occurs near San Francisco at Point Diablo.

❧❧❧

HERON ROOKERIES

Sometimes it's best to be out of style

The herons and their allies, including egrets and ibis, are sometimes considered examples of the "charismatic megafauna"—big animals with endearing qualities. These elegant birds exemplify patience as they stand motionless in the shallows waiting for a fish to swim within reach of their lunge. When they fly, they pass low and create an impressive sight overhead. And they are especially lovely to look at, having lengthy necks and legs, and a calm, regal air about them.

Fashion once decreed that women's hats should be adorned with bird plumage. The long, beautiful feathers of herons were especially sought by the "plumassiers" who prepared feathers for the fashion industry, and none more so than the breeding plumage of white egrets. And because these birds were breeding, the killing of adults often left their young to starve, compounding the damage.

Fortunately, the cruelty of this fad was noticed by some influential monarchs. In 1906 Queen Alexandra announced that she would no longer wear wild feathers, and in 1911 Queen Mary disposed of all her plumed hats. But it was a trendy new hairstyle that really halted this madness—in 1913 Irene Castle introduced the bob and other short haircuts, and these cuts would not support large ornamented hats.

New York Harbor's wading birds suffered beyond being hunted. Because of the general environmental deterioration of their habitat, which reduced the availability of prey fish, these birds disappeared from New York Harbor in the early 1900s. But as water quality improved, the "harbor herons"— a catchall phrase for the entire species array—beginning in

1974 recolonized an archipelago of deserted islands, some of them within sight of Manhattan. Total numbers of nesting green herons; yellow-crowned and black-crowned night herons; great, snowy, and cattle egrets; and glossy ibis rose by about a hundred pairs per year between the mid-1970s and mid-1980s. These urban colonies now constitute about one-quarter of all nesting wading birds between Cape May, New Jersey, and Rhode Island.

Recently, I went on a late-May Audubon Society survey of North Brother Island, offshore from the Bronx in New York's East River, during harbor heron nesting season. Although the island was home to a quarantine hospital in an earlier incarnation (and one that housed a famous patient—Typhoid Mary), today it is a ruins, but also thickly overgrown, forming a luxurious habitat for its herons and other birds. Gulls ruled the rooftops and top floors of the hospital, while the herons occupied snaggly groves of low trees. The heron's large twig nests were easy to find: All we had to do was look for "whitewash"—the buildup of droppings on the forest floor—and then turn our gaze upward. Numbers of eggs and chicks were counted via simple ingenuity—rearview mirrors mounted on poles and held over the nests provided perfect views without greatly disturbing the occupants. It was difficult to fathom such a wild scene in the middle of a great metropolis, but this was just one of many heron rookeries that exist near New York City.

The rookeries of these wading birds are unusual because many species nest together, not in isolation as for most other birds. In areas with variable vegetation, the species are sorted to the extent that the heavier herons or egrets occupy the stronger branches while the lighter species nest on flimsier ones. Where the vegetation is homogeneous, larger species nest on top and smaller ones below.

Well to the north of New York Harbor, a large colony of great blue herons nests on Rustico Island, near Prince Edward Island; another large blue heron colony exists at Nanjemoy Creek near the Potomac River. South of New York, Stone Harbor, in Cape May County, New Jersey, is an important rookery for a variety of wading birds. It's said that at dusk in breeding season the sky is filled with a mix of black-crowned and yellow-crowned night herons taking off to feed and glossy ibis, common, snowy, and American egrets, and little, blue, Louisiana, and green herons sailing in to roost in the trees.

One of the most important heronries along the mid-Atlantic coast is at Pea Patch Island in Delaware. Most numerous among its eight kinds of egrets and herons is the cattle egret. Another cattle egret rookery can be found on Islajo Island, in the marsh just inland of Atlantic City, New Jersey. Cattle egrets are now North America's third most abundant large wading bird, behind only ibis and snowy egrets. But in the early 1900s they weren't even present on the continent. Native to West Africa, they appear to have crossed the relatively narrow gap to eastern South America on their own by the 1880s. They spread slowly, reaching Florida in the 1940s and making their way across eastern North America since then. This successful dispersal is due in part to their adaptability and their use of a niche not occupied by native species. These birds are called cattle egrets for a reason—they often walk behind large grazing animals, picking off the insects disturbed by their passing. But cattle egrets have adopted similar behavior in peopled areas, where they follow behind lawn mowers, tractors, and bulldozers, which are equally, if not more effective at scaring up insects.

Large concentrations of nesting waders also occur in the Chesapeake Bay on Poplar Island and Tangier Island, Maryland, and in Mobjack Bay, Virginia. Drum Island, near Charleston, South Carolina, began as a marsh but became low scrubland when the Army Corps of Engineers dumped dredge spoils there. This made it suddenly favorable for wading birds, and it's now home to a huge glossy ibis colony, with more than token representation by snowy egrets and black-crowned night herons.

The greatest original concentrations of snowy and American egrets and great white herons was in the Everglades and the Florida Keys, but these areas were heavily hunted. Their numbers crashed, and laws were passed to protect them; still, illegal hunting continued. When two wardens were shot by poachers over three years, public outrage at murder over hat decorations helped end the bird slaughter. For various reasons but especially habitat loss, wading bird populations in Florida may still be down to only 5 percent of what they were in the 1930s.

HERRING RUNS
Like salmon, only smaller

Along the coast of New England and Maritime Canada, the annual run of herring is eagerly awaited, in part as a food or bait source, but also as a harbinger of spring. Two "river" herrings make these runs, neither the true and strictly marine sea herring. One, the evocatively named alewife, or gaspereau in Canada, is deeper bodied and ranges farther north. (Alewives were once prized for their scales, which were used by jewelers and display industries as "pearl essence.") The other, with the more pedestrian name of blueback herring, is slimmer and is more of a southern species, although the two herring overlap along much of the Atlantic coast.

Only about one foot in length, these fragile yet driven fish have a life cycle like Atlantic salmon, only in miniature. They spawn well up in freshwater streams and brooks, the young grow larger over several months, and then they migrate to sea, where they spend several years before returning to the same river—and maybe even the same reach in the system where they were born.

Because herring make these runs mainly in small flowages, they can often be sighted gathering in difficult pools or blockages as they attempt to work their way upriver. In earlier times the arrival of easily captured protein in local rivers had deep significance, and the cry "The herring are running" generated great excitement. Portions of streams were leased out to the highest bidders, who set up large shoreside operations, netting herring and packing them in barrels for sale to be salted, smoked, or used as lobster bait. Cape Codders also buried herring to make corn grow tall in otherwise unproductive soil.

Today in many places rules limit catches or prohibit fishing on certain days to ensure that enough fish spawn to sustain the run. New England villages still often keep a part-time "herring warden" on the payroll whose job it is to monitor the run, protect against poachers, and in some instances erect—and later take down—temporary fish ladders to help the fish climb waterfalls. The cultural importance of these fish is obvious from the names of minor rivers: Every second or third in New England seems formally or informally to be called Herring River or Herring Brook. (Thoreau, bemoaning already declining herring runs on Cape Cod, wrote, "There are many Herring Rivers on the Cape; they will, perhaps, be more numerous than herrings soon.") Similarly, in eastern Canada "Gaspereau River" predominates.

The primal nature of these runs, albeit miniaturized, is part of what makes them compelling to watch. In *The Run*, John Hay wrote of a scene at Cape Cod's Stony Brook at a pool with a major inflow and a small "waste stream":

> *The brook below the seining pool was roaring and foaming down. Such was the teeming crowd of alewives trying to swim up the ladder, through the violently heavy flow, that there was a constant falling back, a silver slapping and flapping over the concrete rims of the pools. Farther down, where the waste stream tumbled over a small mountain of rocks, too high for the fish to jump (their limit, on a vertical leap, seems to be not much over two feet), there was a scene to force the heart. Always, a certain number of fish, dividing from those that swam the main stream toward the ladder, would attempt the impossible at this place.*
>
> *Yet here, for all their instinctive valiance, was the insurmountable. Now, as they had done for thousands of years, they tried and failed. White tons of water smashed down over the rocks, but time and time again one fish after another made a quick dash into it and almost flew, hanging with vibrant velocity in the torrent until it was flung back. Many were exhausted and found their way back to the main stream, circling and swimming slowly, and a large number were smashed against the rocks to turn belly up and die, eaten later by young eels, or gulls and herons, as they were taken downstream by the current. Some were wedged in the rocks and could be seen for days as the water gradually tore them apart until they were nothing but white shreds of skin.*

Herring runs are purely a spring phenomenon, and dates when they first show tend to be later to the north. In

The Atlantic Shore, written in the mid-1960s, John Hay and Peter Farb gave April 25 as the date when alewives may be expected in quantity on the north side of Cape Cod and May 10 for Damariscotta, Maine, but in this time of global warming these dates may have already advanced. In tributaries of the Hudson River in New York, river herring may run sporadically between April and June. New York also has a well-known run at a small stream in the Long Island community of North Sea, which can be viewed at high tides between mid-April and early May.

At the Cape Cod Canal alewives can be seen schooling before entering the Bournedale run, a site with a public viewing area and a devoted clan of anglers who pursue the striped bass that are pursuing the herring. So popular is this fishery that the herring are caught by officials and doled out to permitted fishermen, with individuals allowed only a dozen per day. This unique fishery is worth watching—anglers carry their allotment just yards away to homemade live cars that float in the canal and liveline the herring right along the banks to catch impressive-sized stripers. The first surge of herring at Bournedale can be expected near the end of March; the run will last into May, and possibly June.

Polarized sunglasses will help in spotting herring. And don't feel funny about staring into the water from a bridge or bank; fish-watching is gaining respect, much as bird-watching has attained. Indeed, there are at least two books devoted to this arcane activity.

HORSESHOE CRAB SPAWNING EVENTS
Ancient blue bloods

In Delaware Bay so many horseshoe crabs come ashore to spawn at once that Joanna Burger, in *A Naturalist along the*

Jersey Shore, likened it to watching "a massive pot of coffee coming to a boil," by "a sea of dark brown shapes" agitating the water. When populations there are high, it may be possible to view two hundred thousand horseshoe crabs per mile of beach.

Elsewhere, this same phenomenon is not usually as grand, but it can still be compelling. When my daughter Laura was turning seven years old, we held a birthday party at a park near a beach on Long Island Sound. Although my wife and I arranged tugs-of-war, potato sack races, and other amusements, the high point of the affair occurred when someone noticed chains of horseshoe crabs traveling like motorcades through the shallows. Soon Laura and her friends were splashing along the shore, lifting, examining, and often shrieking with delight at the improbable creatures in their own backyard.

A relative of both the spider and the ancient, long-extinct trilobite, the horseshoe crab, *Limulus polyphemus,* has survived with little change since Triassic times—virtually identical animals were chiseled out of the Alps from rock that dates back two hundred million years. From above, the horseshoe crab

looks like a dun helmet with eyes. Two of its eyes are prominent, but this arthropod has seven more: two simple, for-
ward-facing eyes that receive ultraviolet light from the moon,
and five tiny light-receptive organs on its underside. The
horseshoe crab's most familiar feature—that long spike of a
tail—is not a weapon but is used simply to try to right itself if
it flips (and not always quickly or successfully). Horseshoe
crabs range from the Yucatán Peninsula in the Gulf of Mexico to northern Maine. They are a coastal species but have
been caught as far as thirty-five miles offshore.

The peaks of these spawning shows—with numerous females each dragging along one to several males—typically
coincide with evening tides of the full moon, often in sandy
coves that are protected from the surf. The gray-green eggs
are laid in clusters of up to twenty thousand per female, but
at about a thousand at a time, at nest sites along the beach,
usually between the low- and high-tide marks. If you come
across a slight depression in the sand and carefully sweep
away the surface grains, you may find clumps of the sticky
eggs, which measure about twelve to an inch. If you place a
few in clean salt water in your refrigerator, they should
hatch within a few weeks. At this time they are about one-
third of an inch long and tail-less; they bear a remarkable re-
semblance to miniature trilobites.

Horseshoe crabs have or have had an unusual diversity
of uses by humans. Native Americans used their shells as
scoops to bail water from canoes and fashioned their tails
into fishing spear tips. The Lenape Indians near Delaware
Bay buried their nitrogen-rich carcasses as fertilizer, gathering them in great numbers as they spawned in May just in
time for planting season, a technique that was adopted by
early European settlers. New England colonists called them
saucepan fish and fed them to pigs. They have always been

the bait par excellence for commercial eel fishermen—nothing attracts eels like an egg-bearing female horseshoe crab, split in half. Horseshoe crabs were even used as chicken feed, but the practice withered inasmuch as the birds developed an off-putting flavor.

Today the primitive horseshoe crab also serves sophisticated pharmaceutical purposes. Its copper-based blood has only one kind of cell; an enzyme in these cells is widely used to test drugs for bacteria, to inhibit certain cancer cells, and to help diagnose spinal meningitis and gonorrhea. The crabs are captured and brought to laboratories, drained of one-third of their blood, held overnight, and then released alive (with about 10 percent mortality). The sapphire-blue blood is centrifuged to separate white blood cells, and these are ruptured to release a protein, which is eventually converted to a freeze-dried powder called limulus amebocyte lysate or, more commonly, LAL. Pharmaceutical firms pay up to three dollars per crab used in this fashion—about three hundred thousand crabs per year. In 1999 about three million of these once largely ignored relicts were harvested for all purposes, the catch having a value of about three million dollars.

Delaware Bay is the greatest breeding location for horseshoe crabs. The bay is also North America's second largest staging area for about twenty kinds of migratory shorebirds such as red knots and ruddy turnstones, all relying on horseshoe crab eggs to replenish their energy reserves during their trips from South America to their Arctic Circle breeding grounds. "Fishing" for Delaware Bay horseshoe crabs in the old days was not much sport. Watermen and farmers would drive their trucks right onto the beach and flip the biggest animals into barrels and trailers. Some are still harvested for bait, and this has taken its toll on this ecologically pivotal population. Around 1990 an estimated one and a quarter million horseshoe crabs spawned on the beaches of Delaware Bay, laying trillions of eggs vital to the spring hemispheric bird migration. But research showed as much as a 90 percent decline through the 1990s. Many of the birds spend two weeks feasting on the eggs, but in 1999 scientists reported birds departing undernourished, the completion of their long journey in doubt. Accordingly, in August 2000 federal authorities announced plans for an eighteen-hundred-square-mile sanctuary, the Carl N. Schuster Jr. Horseshoe Crab Reserve, with all taking of horseshoe crabs forbidden, from Delaware Bay out into the Atlantic, to protect the rapidly dwindling stocks in the world's prime population region.

At times anywhere along the horseshoe crab's range local beaches may be littered with their shells, suggesting that some great underwater catastrophe occurred. But this is nothing but a natural phenomenon—horseshoe crabs, like true crabs and lobsters, must molt their shells as they grow, and their new shells expand to be about 30 percent larger than the old ones. When this shell shedding happens en masse, the effects can be alarming to those who don't understand this simple fact of life for hard-bodied invertebrates. But if you look closely, you'll see they are just thin shells—"casts" from a mass molting of creatures fitting into their next suit of armor.

HURRICANES

Nature's greatest force meets the coast

Hurricanes account for four of *Weatherwise* magazine's Top Ten U.S. Weather and Climate Events of the Twentieth

Century; its judges ranked the Galveston hurricane of 1900 third, Andrew sixth, Camille seventh, and the 1938 New England hurricane tenth. It is difficult to grasp a hurricane's strength, said by Sebastian Junger in *The Perfect Storm* to be the most powerful event on earth. Junger also wrote that the combined nuclear arsenals of the United States and former Soviet Union don't contain enough energy to keep a hurricane going for one day; a single hurricane has enough energy to provide all the electric power the U.S. needs for three or four years. A hurricane's winds at full strength can blow sand fast enough to strip skin off a body; during the 1935 hurricane gusts surpassed two hundred miles per hour, and people were sandblasted to death. A hurricane when it's still an hour away from the coast may be as loud as a jet taking off.

Certain conditions need to exist to spawn hurricanes. The ocean temperature must be above seventy-eight degrees for enough water to evaporate into the atmosphere. But the warm water also has to be at least two hundred feet deep, because the storms stir up the sea, which can bring hurricane-braking cold water up from the deep. Winds near the ocean must spiral inward, counterclockwise, and the air pulled in must be humid, which provides additional energy. These conditions occur only from the equator to about ten degrees latitude, where the earth's rotation is strong enough to translate them into a whirling storm.

As the spiraling humid air rises, moisture condenses, supporting thunderstorms. Air blowing out of the top of the storm forms high clouds that spread for hundreds of miles, as the system begins to qualify for the term *tropical cyclone*. And as the storm continues to develop, some air begins sinking in the middle, forming a cloud-free core—the famous eye of the hurricane: dry air surrounded by a wall of wind.

Tropical cyclones and hurricanes may drift almost aimlessly over equatorial Atlantic waters, but then bolt northward or westward and strike land. Common landing areas are south Florida and just south of Cape Hatteras. As they move inland, they lose strength but produce torrential rains.

As monstrous as hurricanes may be along the shore, nowadays there is usually enough notice to flee. But boats at sea, especially sailboats, often can't get away fast enough, even with warnings. Years ago, the Law of Storms was developed as a set of guidelines for sailing vessels when unable to escape a hurricane's path based on the reality that a sailboat could not travel against the wind, but only with it. The *dangerous* semicircle of such a storm was that portion in which the circulating wind carried the ship in the same general direction as that of the whole storm, thus prolonging the agony of being caught within the hurricane. The most hazardous section of the dangerous semicircle was the forward quadrant, because a ship running with the wind was actually approaching the center of the storm. The *navigable* semicircle was that in which the wind was blowing in the general direction contrary to that of the storm center, and so the ship was increasing the distance between itself and the storm. Sailors would track the clockwise or counterclockwise manner of the wind in the ship's vicinity to try to figure which semicircle the ship lay in relative to the storm. Even with these guidelines, the losses at sea were sometimes tremendous. The 1919 hurricane, which struck Florida and Texas, claimed less than a hundred lives on land but more than five hundred offshore.

Not only do hurricanes generate frightening waves, but they also lift the sea as a mound of water that travels under and to the right of the eye. As the storm nears land, water piles higher and higher because the seafloor keeps it from flowing away. This dome of water is often fifty to one hundred miles wide. Topped by violent surface waves, the storm surge may wreak a goodly share of the havoc brought about by a hurricane. But not always. Sometimes more damage is done and more lives are lost from interior flooding than from winds and storm surges.

To begin to quantify the spectrum of their forces, hurricanes are placed among the five categories of the Saffir/Simpson scale; this provides disaster agencies a sense of what damage may ensue. Even the most minimal hurricane, Category 1, has winds of seventy-four to ninety-five miles per hour, a four- to five-foot storm surge, and the capability of damaging roads and piers. Damage from a Category 3 storm is extensive, given winds of 111 to 130 miles per hour and a storm surge of nine to twelve feet—large trees and utility poles may be blown down, and coastal homes may be struck by flying debris. Category 5 hurricanes are catastrophic. Winds exceed 155 miles per hour; waters rise more than eighteen feet. Under such forces, buildings overturn, doors blow out, and evacuations are needed as far as five or ten miles inland.

The Galveston hurricane of 1900 was the deadliest natural disaster in U.S. history, killing at least eight hundred people. The account of one eyewitness provides some sense of its force:

> With a raging sea rolling around them, with a wind so terrific none could hope to escape its fury, with roofs being torn away and buildings crumbling . . . men, women and children . . . huddled like rats in the structures. As buildings crumpled and crashed, hundreds were buried under debris, while thousands were thrown into the waters, some to meet instant death, oth-

*ers to struggle for a time in vain, and yet thousands to escape
death in miraculous and marvelous ways.*

Ironically, the barricade of wreckage that formed probably limited damage from the surge and waves. The Texas
city took that lesson to heart and built a seawall to protect
against future storms.

Hurricane Camille arrived in August 1969 and topped
out at more than two hundred miles per hour—the highest
winds ever recorded in a North American hurricane. They
blew away the Mississippi coastal highway, hotels, super-
markets, restaurants, quays, and piers. More than two
hundred people died, including an entire group of friends
who assembled in a seafront apartment to hold a "hurricane party."

The New England hurricane plowed through the Northeast in late September 1938. Residents were almost totally
unprepared for it. The weather bureau later calculated that
the storm traveled the 425 miles from North Carolina to
New York in less than seven hours, at an average rate of
more than 65 miles per hour—blazing speed for a hurricane.
Winds from this storm reached 186 miles per hour near
Boston. Survivors reported a wall of water on Long Island's
south shore that was at least thirty feet high. Small boats
were deposited on streets, rowboats ended up in trees, salt
spray was even found on windows in Vermont, and six hundred lives were lost.

For fans of violent storms, the near-term future is
bright—scientists believe that the Atlantic Ocean has
shifted into its alternate warmer phase and, because of this,
strong hurricanes will be more than twice as likely to form
in the next twenty or thirty years than they were between
1970 and the mid-1990s.

∽∾∽

ICEBERGS
Arctic vagrants

Icebergs break off or "calve" from freshwater glaciers. The ice that forms them is from compacted snow that may have accumulated over thousands of years. Due to their high densities they ride low in the water, with only about one-eighth of an iceberg's mass visible above the sea surface; unseen portions are as dangerous to mariners as rock reefs. And it's no wonder they don't yield to ships—large icebergs may weigh as much as a million and a half tons. Smallish chunks are called growlers; those to the size of a small house are known as bergy bits. Larger than that, they are full-fledged bergs.

Arctic icebergs shrink in size as they drift south. Where the air is considerably warmer than the sea, they retain their stability and, as their bulk decreases, gradually rise out of the water, leaving telltale rings of former waterlines. Where the sea temperature is warmer than the air, icebergs melt faster below the waterline and become unstable, often rotating to find new equilibria. Wave action at the waterline girdles icebergs, cold air solidifies them, and all these processes cause them to emit weird sounds as if the ice is alternately being contracted and expanded.

Shortly before midnight on April 14, 1912, the *Titanic* steamed ahead at full speed toward a North Atlantic ice field seventy miles long and twelve miles wide, ignoring messages from other ships about the danger and even iceberg sightings by its own lookout from the crow's nest. When the lookout warned of an iceberg immediately ahead, the first officer attempted to change course. But it was too late. Although the ice mass was not large, a knifelike protrusion ripped a three-hundred-foot gash in the hull well below the waterline. Two hours later the "unsinkable" ship lay on the ocean bottom.

It's estimated that about fifteen thousand icebergs calve from Arctic glaciers each year. The Labrador Current sweeps down from Baffin Island and northern Greenland with its cargo of white megaliths and is known as Iceberg Alley. Most icebergs in the North Atlantic originate from the west coast of Greenland, where about a hundred glaciers from the island's ice cap spawn bergs, mainly in summer.

Few make it as far south as Newfoundland, although some can be seen into July off that province. In an average year about four hundred icebergs drift below the forty-eighth parallel, with about thirty-five making it past the tail of the Grand Banks to threaten the transatlantic shipping lanes. Annual variation in their appearances is great; in 1958 only 1 iceberg was seen south of forty-eight degrees latitude, while the next year 693 were in evidence. Freak traverses took place in 1907 and 1926 when combinations of winds and currents drove some as far south as Bermuda.

❧

ICHTHYOSARCOTOXISM
Russian roulette fish appetizers

Eating fugu is the culinary version of Russian roulette. *Fugu* is the generic name for puffers in Japan, where they are considered the tastiest of fish. But while the roundish puffers look innocuous, deadly tetrodotoxin (more than a thousand times more potent than cyanide) may be contained in their liver, gonads, intestines, and, in some species, the skin. All of this introduces a certain thrill to a fish appetizer—the risk of ichthyosarcotoxism, or fish-flesh poisoning. One species is so associated with this phenomenon in Japanese waters that it is known as *maki-maki:* the death puffer.

The somewhat perverse place of fugu in Japanese culture is summed up in the traditional expression: "Those who eat fugu soup are stupid. But those who don't eat fugu soup are also stupid." A gourmet once wrote, "The taste of fugu is incomparable. If you eat it three or four times, you are enslaved. Anyone who declines it for fear of death is really a pitiable person." Nonetheless, fugu is the only delicacy that cannot be served to the emperor of Japan and his family, so as to avoid their being added to the seventy to one hundred lives that are lost to it each year.

Fugu commands the highest food prices in Japan, partly because it is a status symbol and because specially trained cooks must be hired to prepare it. But when a mistake is made, the consequences can be ghastly. The nervous system is attacked by the curarelike poison, and victims suffer respiratory distress, tremors, paralysis, and convulsions. The fatality rate is about 60 percent, and death, when it occurs, is usually within twenty-four hours. For American culinary risk takers who don't want to travel to Japan, fugu is imported to the United States.

Toxic puffers also have a more practical use. Steinbeck and Ricketts in *The Sea of Cortez* told of offering to buy a puffer from a boy in Baja California. But the boy refused, ". . . saying that a man had commissioned him to get this fish and he was to receive ten centavos for it because the man wanted to poison a cat."

Ciguatera is another form of fish-flesh poisoning that can be fatal, and is produced by as many as four hundred varieties of tropical marine fish. Although the word *ciguatera* is derived from the Spanish name for a poisonous snail, the disease was first reported as being fish-toxin based in 1555 from the West Indies.

Ciguatera's symptoms are decidedly unpleasant, or worse. A tingling sensation on the lips, tongue, or throat may occur within as short a time as two to three hours, or as long as a day, after eating the contaminated fish. Paradoxical sensory disturbances may ensue; cold may feel like burning and hot objects may seem cold. Numbness is usually accompanied by nausea, abdominal cramps, vomiting, and diarrhea. The muscles of the mouth may become drawn and spastic, and pain and looseness may be felt in the teeth. The victim feels progressively weaker, with muscular pain in the arms and legs. Vision can become blurry or temporarily cease. Skin eruptions often occur. In severe cases the victim has difficulty walking and may lose muscular coordination or become paralyzed. Although the fatality rate is about 10 percent, survivors may require many months to recuperate.

Until 1965, there was no known antidote for ciguatera poisoning, but since then medications have become available. But the best action is avoidance. It is not caused by spoiled fish, and may be transmitted by perfectly fresh and otherwise edible specimens. Particularly troublesome is that it can erupt from a species that was previously known to be edible in a specific locality or in a species that's commonly eaten in other regions with no history of ciguatera intoxications.

The ultimate source of the toxin is a bottom-dwelling blue-green alga. Typically, grazing fish species not consumed by humans feed on this alga, and they in turn are fed upon by predatory fishes harvested by people. Some of the predatory fish have small home ranges and either do or don't encounter prey species harboring the toxin, and so certain rules of thumb emerge as to eating them. Thus, barracuda on one side of Grand Cayman Island are considered safe, whereas those from the other side are not consumed. The most common ciguatera-producing fish in U.S. waters are the great barracuda, yellowfin grouper, red snapper, and great amberjack. As a rule, you should never eat the liver, intestines, or roe of tropical marine fish.

Besides puffers, a few groups of fish have their own poisonous-flesh syndromes. Tropical herring and shad, members of the family Clupeidae, may harbor clupeotoxin, which has killed humans in less than fifteen minutes. Scombroid poisoning occurs from eating tuna and mackerel that have been poorly preserved. A particular bacterium produces symptoms resembling histamine intoxication, including intense headaches, dizziness, throat burning, and difficulty in breathing. Fortunately, sensitive palates can detect the sharp or peppery taste that signals an afflicted fish.

Some seafood sources that are more evolutionarily advanced than fish may be poisonous, among them sea turtles, the flesh of which can bring on a frightening array of nasty symptoms. Many of them are focused on the mouth, which becomes tingly and stiff and gives off very foul breath, while the tongue develops a white coating and becomes covered with reddened papules, which turn into ulcers. Almost half of the stricken expire. A strange form of poisoning—one unlikely to occur often today—stems from eating the liver and kidneys of polar bears. The high concentrations of vitamin A contained in them bring on a litany of symptoms, including headaches, nausea, dizziness, convulsions, and collapse. Although no fun to live through, fatalities are rare.

JELLYFISH
Beautiful stingers

"Behold the lion's mane!" cried Sherlock Holmes as he revealed the murderer in "The Adventure of the Lion's Mane"; in this Arthur Conan Doyle story, that particular jel-

lyfish was said to be more deadly than a cobra—a gross exaggeration. Nonetheless, they do deserve respect—a jellyfish's sting can cause symptoms ranging from slight discomfort all the way to agonizing pain.

Jellyfish, graceful ghosts of the sea, are for the most part well armed for creatures that are about 93 percent water. Stinging threads are contained within specialized cells called nematocysts arrayed along their tentacles like poisonous harpoons. Jellyfish feed by snaring passing prey with these appendages, which then contract, drawing food to the mouth. Some jellyfish capture and consume relatively large fish and even other jellyfish.

Jellyfish are a summertime problem—not only because that is when they are most abundant but also because that is when the greatest numbers of people are in the water. Lifeguard lore has it that their numbers reflect water temperatures: The more tepid, the more jellyfish appear. Even if this is true, prevailing winds and currents also play large roles in dictating where they accumulate and become a problem.

The lion's mane is the most common species along much of the East and Gulf Coasts. It is the largest of all jellyfish—specimens eight feet wide have been found. Typically, though, it has a six- to eight-inch bell and a short, dangling, reddish mop. The lion's mane can inflict serious damage to those who are unfortunate enough to be struck in the eye by its microscopic lances or who are allergic to its toxins.

In early summer swimmers on northeastern beaches may feel a sharp sting that chases them out of the water—victims of sea nettles. Common from North Carolina to Long Island, sea nettles are a small, lacy, white- or red-striped jellyfish. In some years, particularly in the Chesapeake Bay, they abound and make swimming impossible for a time. But it pays to search among potential bathing beaches; because sea nettles are poor swimmers, they are at the mercy of currents, which may clear them from some locations and concentrate them in others.

Another common jellyfish along Atlantic shores is the moon jelly, which is from three to ten inches wide and easily identified by the four conspicuous whitish, horseshoe-shaped gonads located toward the center of its bell. Although the sting of this jellyfish is too weak to be sensed, they are an unusual source of annoyance. At times they appear in high densities. When water-skiers pass through these aggregations, the moon jellies get sucked into the boat's propellers and are sprayed back into its wake, pelting the water-skiers with what feels like Jell-O. Dying moon jellies often wash up on shores in large numbers; this is a normal part of their life cycle in which their larvae detach from the parents and settle into the shore zone to spend the winter in the polyp stage, attached to the bottom like a mushroom.

In the Gulf of Mexico cannonball jellyfish may become phenomenally abundant. These three- to six-pound purple and white balls can blanket the water when conditions are right. Once when conditions were very right, someone estimated that two million per hour were passing down the channel at Port Aransas, Texas. And the cannonballs have new, even larger company—the twenty-five pound Australian spotted jellyfish is now firmly established in the gulf.

The Pacific coast has a two-inch-long jellyfish, *Vellela lata,* that is much appreciated by beachcombers. Because they are an open-sea species, when they strike the shore it indicates the presence of offshore waters that may also carry Japanese glass floats and other highly regarded artifacts. The strandings of this jellyfish may be massive enough to create a light blue plasma belt along the high-tide line, which can be a walking hazard due to its extreme slipperiness.

As a rule, efforts to keep stinging jellyfish away from beaches don't work. When in the summer of 1999, a two-thousand-dollar experimental net designed to separate bathing children from jellyfish at a beach in Hampton Bays, New York, failed, plans were scrapped to erect a larger, more costly net the following year. Although most whole jellyfish were kept out in the experiment, wave action pushed pieces of dead ones through the mesh. Unfortunately, the stingers of jellyfish remain active long after the animal dies.

Experts recommend that if you're stung, treatment should include peeling off the tentacles with a stick or other foreign object, drying the skin but without rubbing, and applying dry sand, vinegar, or, believe it or not, a meat tenderizer. Freshwater rinses should be avoided—their low salt content increases the osmotic pressure inside any nematocysts remaining on the flesh, thereby inducing discharge of the stinging threads.

JUBILEES

Fishing doesn't come easier

When a very particular set of weather and tidal conditions occurs in summer, seafood lovers near the east shore of Mobile Bay, near Daphne, Alabama, take notice. The subtle cues are these: The previous day must have been overcast, there must be a continuing gentle east wind, and the tide must be rising. If this situation holds, they get down to the beach before sunrise: Fish and crabs may literally be leaping and crawling on shore, while the immediate shallows are brimming with life.

These marine jubilees can be as festive for seafood gatherers as the name suggests. Natives cry *Jubilee!* and word spreads; soon masses of people are working the shore, buckets, baskets, gigs, and nets in hand. Most of the bounty of fish is made up of bottom dwellers, such as flounder, marine catfish, and stingrays. Crustaceans include shrimp and blue crabs. Jubilees have been noted in Mobile Bay since about 1860. So ingrained are they in the

local culture that the Junior League of Mobile has published a 750-recipe cookbook for preparing the harvest called *Recipe Jubilee*.

But despite the fun that is had, the phenomenon does not represent a happy ecological circumstance. Jubilees are caused by upwellings or upslope movements of deeper oxygen-poor waters, which drives bottom-dwelling animal life before it. The oxygen is depleted by the decomposition of detritus and plankton. By the time this band of deoxygenated water reaches the shore, it has concentrated vast numbers of sea creatures, which become pinned between two environments they can't live in. A falling tide or a shift in wind will break a Mobile Bay jubilee, however, and rescue the animals.

Less celebrated jubilees can occur in other locations. Once I witnessed this phenomenon in a bay of Long Island Sound. Arriving at the beach to fish for snapper bluefish, I immediately saw that something was very wrong. The shallows were littered with crabs, young lobsters, pipefish, a few large flounder that I could pick up with my hands, and countless numbers of young-of-the-year flounder. The baby flounder were so dense that they lay side to side, fitting together like an Escher print, and they pummeled my legs as I waded. Local seabirds had it easy, eating their fill of the little fish. Fortunately, the wind shifted, reversing the upwelling, and these denizens of the deep waters of the harbor fled to their normal haunts.

∾∾∾

LIGHT AND THE SEA
A beguiling interplay

Francis Bacon wrote, "The beholding of the light is itself a more excellent and a fairer thing than all the uses of it."

But light is the most critical aspect of life—our food chains are based directly on converting the energy of the sun's rays through photosynthesis, yet light can be subtle, entrancing, and amorphous. This elusive nature of light also frustrates; Benjamin Franklin once wrote: "I am much in the dark about light." I believe light often is best appreciated in the presence of water. The wonderfully varied synergisms of these media stem from a host of interactions that are based on pure physics—but that yield sublime aesthetics. And nowhere do aqua and terra dazzle in more ways than along the coast, where water comes in so many forms that play with light: choppy, blue waves; rolling turquoise combers; white, foamy breakers; placid tide pools; murky brownish estuaries; silvery sheets of sea ice; and gray fogs that seem to swallow the sun. All the same substance, but in varied forms with radically different personalities.

Despite Franklin's declaration, much about light is known—for instance, why the seas are colored. Rachel Carson wrote, "The deep blue water of the open sea far from land is the color of emptiness and barrenness; the green water of the coastal areas, with all its varying hues, is the color of life." The deep water is blue because as light rays journey downward through it, the red rays and most of the yellow ones are absorbed, leaving the cool blue light to be reflected to our eyes. But where the water is rich with plankton, as usually occurs along the coast, light can't penetrate as far, and a greenish cast results.

Even something as seemingly simple as the local color of water is dictated by the angle and intensity of the illumination, the depth and clarity of the water, and three pathways for the light: reflection from the water's surface, refraction through the surface of light scattered from the volume of water itself, and reflections from the bottom that are refracted from the surface. The relative contributions of each source shift with the circumstances. In shallow water, light from the bottom is most important; in deep clear water, surface reflections are brightest. And in muddy water, light is primarily scattered by the very sediments that cloud the water.

When sunlight reflects from mildly dimpled water, we may see skypools—inky or iridescent oblong patches that dance with the waves. A caustic network is the pattern of irregular and shiny lines that reflect or refract from an undulating water surface. These are the constantly wavering light bands you see on a swimming pool on a bright day, or in clear sandy shallows, or reflected off the polished sides of a boat.

Glitter is another coastal light phenomenon—that ribbon of sparkling light visible over wind-ruffled water when the sun or moon is at a low angle to the horizon. These instantaneous flashes of reflected sunlight form an ensemble of countless glints. It can be a glorious segue to the day's final act—a line of light linking the observer to the sunset—but when the orb reaches the horizon the glitter fades, leaving all attention on the sinking star.

Rough seas can generate light phenomena. Rainbows are associated with sunlight shining through the soggy atmosphere of a passing thunderstorm. But "surf bows" form in the mist over a large breaking surf. Under the right conditions, a rainbow may meet a surf bow, extending the arc of color below the horizon. Rarely, "fog bows" can be seen, although typically the small droplets of the mist yield only pale colors.

Sometimes when viewing the sea from on high, you can see broad light-colored areas. These are usually from oil slicks—not of the Exxon *Valdez* kind, but natural surface films from fat-bearing organisms. Even this incredibly thin coating takes energy from waves and dampens them, smoothing out the water. Smooth water reflects more light than agitated water, so slicks form bright spots on the sea.

Although large amounts of spilled petroleum become unequivocal ecological tragedies, small amounts of oil had practical value for mariners. Seamen in dories attempting to land on wave-battered beaches sometimes tossed oil in the water to pacify the surf. And Cape Codders in search of sea clams would drip small amounts of oil around their skiffs to calm the surface so they could see more clearly through the depths.

Some of the most spectacular shows of light and water are put on twice per day in the routine rising and setting of the sun. A sun-on-the-horizon phenomenon, the "green flash," was thought fictitious by some. But a scientist demonstrated that this flash can occur when conditions are just right. These include a haze-free and cloudless view of the sun at sunrise or sunset. Refraction of light rays may allow a green, wavering spot lasting for about thirty seconds near the top or slightly above the star. Far less common is an actual bright green flash.

One old New Jersey bayman articulated the advantage to watching a coastal sunrise, saying, "You got to be on the bay to see a day born; back on the mainland you just see the sun come up."

LOOMINGS

Seeing beyond the limits

With eyes situated at or a little above sea level, the ocean appears vast, but the view is greatly limited by the

curvature of the earth that produces that natural border—
the horizon. A person about five feet tall can see about two
and a half miles distant. Additional elevation of the observer rapidly increases the area seen, as does elevation of
the object viewed. With eyes at ten feet, you can see four
and a half miles away. And standing on the shore, the five-
foot person can see a sixteen-foot-high sailboat from more
than seven miles.

In clear, stable weather the bend in the earth sets the
boundaries of vision. But water causes light to refract—to
bend—and often the air over the sea holds enough moisture
to toy with light beams over long distances. If an object is
near the horizon, this bending of light may cause the object
to warp, magnify, or even turn upside down in what have
long been known as loomings. Of course, these almost supernatural manifestations demanded explanation; in one
medieval legend, they were conjured by Fata Morgana, a marine enchantress, whose position undersea was marked by
the locations of the distortions. John Stilgoe, in *Alongshore*,
pointed out that not every ship sailing off to the horizon
vanishes in stages, but rather looming sometimes makes a
ship appear to topple, possibly "confirming" theories that
the world ends at a definite edge.

John Brocklesby, in *Elements of Meteorology*, was the
first to thoroughly explain looming as an optical mix of
refraction and reflection, and he distinguished between
instances in which an object before or on the horizon appears to be lifted as simple looming, and the more magical extraordinary looming. Among the extraordinary are
instances when objects seen are *beyond* the horizon, and
sometimes inverted. In 1822, for example, a captain recognized his father's ship by an upside-down image in the
air, despite the fact that it was thirty miles distant and,

even more astonishingly, seventeen miles beyond the horizon.

Howard Shannon, in *The Book of the Seashore,* a natural history of the ocean side of Long Island, New York, wrote about a consistently observed looming from the section of coast known as Long Beach that Brocklesby certainly would have called extraordinary. On dry clear days, no land whatsoever can be seen from that shore. But under certain conditions the otherwise invisible Atlantic Highlands of New Jersey, seventeen nautical miles across the New York Bight, loom clearly into view. Shannon described these conditions as including cloudy elements in that quarter of the lower sky; if air layers of greatly varying density develop in what appears to be the clearest weather so as to create the effect of a great lens, then light rays may be refracted—that is, bent in a huge bow.

Shannon wrote of witnessing this looming on a clear and virtually cloudless August day, but under a sky that presumably held some moisture, probably increasing as the day progressed:

> . . . one floating white cloud hinted at disturbed densities there. Yet unseen but potent influences were obviously at work. For those emergent blue hills and all their lesser fellows, which now slowly rose from their one-time hidden place and grew higher as the afternoon advanced—and clearer, too—finally stood forth along the southwestern horizon as a many-hilled but low-lying silhouette of purest azure that seemed actually afloat in the sunlit summer atmosphere.

Locals, familiar with the looming of the highlands, claimed it presaged rain within twenty-four hours, which is consistent with the trend toward humidity. Shannon also said that New York City's already towering skyline sometimes becomes visible from incredible distances owing to this phenomenon, and that from shore, steamers may undergo curious distortions in which superstructures magnify themselves until the grotesque vessel seems three times its normal height. Today's cliché that something is "looming on the horizon" gains new meaning when it regains old meaning.

ᘏᘏᘏ

MANATEES

Mermaid from afar, not so lovely near

Some think that manatees are at the root of mermaid stories. Perhaps if you squint really hard at these sluggish and homely seal-like mammals, you'll see the basis for this belief. Or maybe you need to be an exhausted, female-deprived sailor of yesteryear.

Despite their appearance, manatees are more closely related to elephants than seals. The original range of manatees, also known as sea cows, was from south Texas to the Florida Keys, and northward to the Carolinas. Only about two thousand of the now federally endangered manatees remain in United States today, mostly in Florida. Their decrease in numbers is due mainly to habitat loss and propeller wounds from motorboats. Manatees had a particularly bad time in 1996—four hundred died, the most in twenty-two years, and nearly double the previous record. Not only did powerboats exact their toll that year, but a toxic red algal bloom killed at least 158 that had wintered in the warm water near a power plant in the Caloosahatchee

River and then swam into the red tide as they moved down-river in spring.

Manatees usually inhabit creeks and backwaters, in-cluding along the Intracoastal Waterway. In these quiet places individuals graze from sixty to a hundred pounds of grasses per day. Manatees are only moderately social, at times living alone or in small groups—but they were some-times seen in great herds in times of their native abun-dance. They cavort when they meet, embracing each other with their flippers and even pressing their lips together in a gesture resembling a kiss.

Manatees are not often seen in the ocean, although I once spotted two adults and a pup that were traveling south just outside the surf in Fort Lauderdale, Florida, during a cold snap. The little herd could easily have passed under the long ocean-fishing pier I was standing on, but some instinct caused them to swim all around its perimeter, allowing me a prolonged once-in-a-lifetime view.

In 1995 a ten-foot-long twelve-hundred-pounder nick-named Chessie traveled past through Long Island Sound all the way to Point Judith, Rhode Island, before turning around and heading south. In 1998 another vagrant man-atee made itself known when it was spotted in Montauk Harbor, New York, by a guest in a shorefront hotel. Florida manatees also sometimes range westward to Louisiana.

Particularly reliable locations in Florida to see manatees include the Suwanee, Homosassa, Crystal, and St. Johns Rivers, and at Everglades National Park and Cape Canaveral. During cold periods in winter, manatees sometimes congre-gate in the warm outflows of electric-generating stations, where they can be easily observed.

The manatees of Florida are one of only four kinds in its taxonomic order worldwide. A fifth, the Steller's sea cow—another North American species—appears to be extinct, and its rapid eradication shows just how important an effective Endangered Species Act is. The Steller's sea cow measured up to twenty-eight feet long and weighed as much as eight tons. These kelp eaters had stout forelimbs and a whalelike tail and lived in Arctic waters off Alaska and the Russian Far East.

Biologists believe the total population size of the Steller's sea cow was about two thousand when Western explorers began to kill them for food and for their hides. The huge, easily hunted beasts enabled a shipwrecked crew off the coast of Kamchatka to survive and return home. By 1768 it was extinct, just twenty-seven years after the naturalist George Steller described the species. But maybe not. Since then, there have been occasional reports suggesting that small colonies might have survived in remote areas. In the mid-1800s such reports were not unusual, and in 1962, the crew of a Russian whaler reported seeing six animals resembling sea cows feeding in a bay. In 1977 a fisherman in Kamchatka told of actually touching a drifting animal that matched the description of a sea cow. One can only hope that one of nature's most unusual beasts is holding on somewhere in a distant sanctuary.

MISCELLANEOUS BEACH FINDS
Some natural, some not

There is something wonderfully atavistic in scouring shores for the endless array of items the sea can deliver. Sometimes you'll find articles of *flotsam* and *jetsam*. These two old English words, which refer to humankind's possessions, are often confused. *Flotsam* are items that have floated away, but not by design; *jetsam* are things thrown overboard or jettisoned. But then there is the even greater universe of oddities that the oceans naturally yield. Together, the objects both man-made and nature-born make beaches well worth combing, by anyone from children outfitted with the classic pail and shovel to semiprofessionals who collect and deal their discoveries.

In colonial times beachcombing in places such as Cape Cod was one way of finding essential natural materials and earning a living by finding marketable flotsam and jetsam. Thoreau wrote of how after an easterly storm in spring, the Cape Cod's outer beach was sometimes strewn with logs from Maine from one end to the other—a godsend for the inhabitants of a sandy peninsula nearly destitute of wood. Professional beachcombers on Cape Cod and elsewhere were known as wreckers because much of what they found was the cargo of the frequent shipwrecks that occurred. Thoreau called the wrecker "the true monarch of the beach" whose "right there is none to dispute." Social protocols evolved to claim large, hard-to-move spoils—a stone placed on a find served as an honored deed of security.

Today it is the hobbyist who rules, but the spoils are less dramatic. In Maine painted wooden lobster buoys would constitute an exemplary find; most existing examples are now in antiques shops or private collections, having been replaced with cheap Styrofoam floats. Although the plastic floats also are collected, they lack the rich patina of distressed paint and salt-bleached wood that the older buoys offer.

In eastern Long Island where I often surf cast, I find many bones of large fish along the shore—whole skulls of striped bass, bluefish, and other gamefish left behind from fishermen who've beheaded their catches on the beach or who've thrown fish remains off their boats. These skeletons become cleaned in the ocean waters, eventually washing up and mixing with seaweeds on the high shore. Sometimes they remain largely articulated with backbones in place, ready to be gathered up gently and perhaps glued to a board and hung outside a beach house. But more often you find individual, glistening white vertebral segments, gill flaps, and lower jaws, which add a dimension to beach glass displays and other shore finds. A special fish bone find, a "crucifix," is sometimes seen at Cape Canaveral. This skull of a marine catfish is white, intricate in design, and, as the name implies, resembles Christ on the cross. The barbed tail spines of stingrays are another interesting possibility.

Routinely found in Florida and the shores of other southern states are chunks of coral in various colors and forms. But there is a northern coral that ranges *south* to Florida—the star or northern coral, found all the way to Massachusetts. Sponges may also be seen along much of the Atlantic coast, including "deadman's fingers," shaped like digits, and redbeard sponge, which also looks like its name suggests it should. Then there are sand dollars—actually modified sea urchins that when perished, are found as flat white discs on the beach and kept as souvenirs.

Common along the Atlantic are small, puffy black "maiden's purses" with four wispy tails. These are the empty egg cases of skates (relatives of rays and sharks) that have become detached from their subtidal anchorages. The two longer tendrils supply the developing skate with oxygen, while the shorter ones remove wastes. Another frequently seen egg case is produced by whelks. These look like strings of creamy- or yellow-colored discs. Each circle-bead holds many eggs embedded in a jelly, but they'll loosen up and rattle when dried.

On the north shore of Long Island, New York, it's not hard to find "Indian Paint Pots," roundish mineral formations that resemble cups. Their high concentrations of iron oxide give them a reddish cast; when used as a pestle with a mortar and a little water, a brownish red paste can be formed that is said to have been used by Native Americans as body paint.

A prize find on any coast is ivory or whalebone. Ivory appears mainly on Alaskan beaches in the form of walrus tusks and sperm whale teeth. Whalebone has a wider distribution, but be aware of regulations concerning possession of ivory and whalebone.

Ardently collected all around North America are beach glass and beach pottery. Fresh examples of each are sharp edged; those that have been tossed about by the sea are rounded and polished, and are far more desirable. Beach glass and pottery are more numerous around heavily populated regions, but there is hardly a shore anywhere that doesn't hold at least a few examples. For beach glass, "frosty clear" is the most common, the powdery finish coming from abrasion. More highly prized are translucent colors, with green and brown predominating, and red, yellow, and blue being rarer. Some may be so well shaped and polished as to resemble gemstones.

The Pacific coast has a serious beachcombing following—and with good reason: It borders and receives some of what washes up from the world's largest ocean, at seventy-one million square miles. This great size, combined with large human populations living on northern Pacific Ocean shores, weather patterns that move westward over the ocean, and felicitous currents, all make North America's Pacific coast arguably the best beachcombing reach in the world.

Most important in carrying flotsam and jetsam to the West Coast is the Japan Current or Kuroshio (meaning "black stream," for its dark shading). This flow delivers a vast array of Oriental items, some of which are particularly prized by collectors. Among these are large Japanese sake jugs, sought by interior decorators.

Much of the material that makes Pacific beachcombing so special is derived from commercial fishing operations of the United States and Canada, along with Russia, Japan, and other Asian nations. Among this category are Japanese tuna line lights (to illuminate strings of hook-bearing lines that may be fifty miles long), Russian steel net floats, crab pots (often with crabs inside) and cedar crab pot floats, and woven bamboo fishing gear trays. Commercial shipping also yields a great deal of marked Oriental wood dunnage (the lumber used to protect cargo and provide spaces between cargoes for tie-down). Highly regarded finds on the West Coast and everywhere else are pieces of shipwrecks, particularly portal and hatch covers and labeled life rings.

Especially prized and collected are glass floats used to suspend nets by Japanese fishermen. These floats are hand-blown in numerous colors and sizes and are usually encased in manila hemp mesh. One devotee estimates that there are more than twelve million of these floats in use in the Pacific. Long Beach Peninsula in Washington catches huge amounts of drift from the Japan Current. At that beach, one professional beachcomber, using a car on the heels of a storm in 1963, set what may be the record for collecting Japanese glass fishing floats: 220 of them in one tide. Such is the passion with which these are sought on West Coast shores that there is even a guidebook devoted to this beachcombing specialty.

The Pacific coast beachcombing network has also recognized broad episodic strandings, usually connected with particular mishaps at sea. A considerable amount of Spanish beeswax of late-1600s manufacture and possibly connected with a Spanish galleon that disappeared in 1705 somehow was buried in the beach sand on the ocean side of the Nehalem Sand Spit in Oregon; sizable chunks turned up through the 1930s, and small pieces are still found today. Around 1960 sealed ginger jars washed up in profusion on the Oregon and Washington coasts. In 1969 twelve-inch mercury thermometers showed up on Oregon shores. And there was an invasion of three-inch red plastic toys over miles of beach on the Queen Charlotte Islands of British Columbia.

Any Pacific shore is worth scouting, but some beaches have well-earned reputations as beachcombing hot spots. In California these include Newport, Santa Monica, and Ventura Beaches in southern California, Morro Bay and Monterey Bay in the central part of the state, and in northern California from Point Reyes north past Crescent City. Oregon's mostly sandy beaches are easily accessible; good beachcombing locations include Gold Beach, Bandon, Coos Bay Spit, Winchester Bay, Yachats, Lincoln City, Tillamook Bay's south spit, and Seaside. Huge quantities of collectible driftwood pile up at Oregon's Battle Rock State Park. Washington's beaches are not as easily reached as Oregon's. Southern Washington offers a few excellent locations, such as Long Beach, Grayland, Ocean Shores, Copalis, and Pacific Beach. Annual beachcombers' fairs, complete with competitions for finds in various categories, are held in Bandon, Netarts, and Seaside, Oregon, and in Grayland, Washington.

British Columbia's coast consists mainly of rugged, rocky inlets, but where beaches exist they are rewarding. The province offers a specialty on Texada Island—beautiful mottled "flower rocks" of greenish porphyrite. Alaskan beaches are near-virgin territory for beachcombing, and most can be reasonably reached only by floatplane. Nonetheless, some pilots do beachcomb the rich Alaskan beaches, some-times landing on flat sand or nearby lakes and even anchor-ing their planes offshore and rafting in.

Those wanting to jump into beachcombing with a flourish might heed the advice of author Amos Wood, who cited four hot spot areas for the Pacific coast: Baja, Mexico; Nehalem Spit, Oregon; Graham Island, British Columbia; and Port Heiden, Alaska.

Making truly special finds while beachcombing is not a high-probability endeavor. As such, you should heed cer-tain simple principles: Coves are better than points of land; places where general detritus washes up, especially drift-wood and kelp, are likely to also harbor treasures; and on-shore winds are better than offshore winds. Indeed, onshore winds of fifteen miles an hour persisting for fifteen hours or more will usually carry in ocean drift riches.

But even as seemingly a placid activity as beachcombing has dangers (beyond greenhead flies, sunburns, and rogue waves). Every once in a while a potentially still live World War II mine that has been circling the Kuroshio Current washes up on a Pacific shore.

∾∾∾

MONARCH BUTTERFLY FLIGHTS
Unlikely coastal migrants

The remarkable annual migration of monarch butter-flies is not strictly a coastal event. Nonetheless, perhaps using the shoreline as a marker, fluttering monarchs can at times overwhelm the seaside landscape.

Monarch butterflies make one of the most dramatic mass movements in the insect world. Each winter individu-als drawn from all over North America settle into oyamel fir forests in a small region of Mexico that has the particular

microclimate monarch butterflies prefer. On the Plain of Mule, Altamirano Hill, and other forested harbors ten thousand feet above sea level, millions of the lovely monarchs cling to tree trunks, layered like tarnished gold. In March they leave these few dozen acres for points north. Along the way three generations of females lay their eggs on milkweed plants. It is only the fourth-generation butterflies that return, purely by instinct, to a place they've never been.

It is the migration of this fourth cohort that charms seaside strollers in early autumn. These monarchs lack the speed or elevation of southbound hawks and falcons. At an average rate of nine miles an hour and seventy to ninety miles per day, the migration from northern locales two thousand miles distant from the wintering roost may require a month. The scale of this movement can be staggering; researchers in New Jersey estimated that 136,000 to 384,000 monarchs were passing per hour per square mile at the height of the migration in 1999. Streams of monarchs extend southward, and they can often be seen fluttering many miles offshore over the Gulf of Mexico as they head toward the mountains of central Mexico. It's believed that millions perish at this stage, sometimes trapped in tropical storms, hurricanes, and other nasty forms of weather. And every now and then the captains and crew of Gulf of Mexico shrimp boats are treated to the sight of their vessel being decorated with hundreds of the exhausted insects as they settle for a rest.

In the Long Island, New York, area the peak of the monarch migration along offshore barrier islands occurs in mid-September. Sometimes after a September cold front, Fire Island on Long Island's south shore hosts thousands of monarchs flying about its dunes. Cape May, New Jersey, is a superb viewing location where the butterflies may pause before crossing the wide expanse of Delaware Bay. They don't fly at night and so can be found roosting in particular trees, often by the hundreds. Although some are seen at Cape May as early as mid-August, the peak occurs over the second half of September. Some years they reach as many as fifteen hundred per hour passing over the hawk-watch site. The butterflies arrive in waves in the warm air that precedes cold fronts, and then flit about locally and roost to wait out the cold before attempting their sea passage. Another great location at Cape May is Pavilion Circle near Cape May Point, which is planted with bushes attractive to monarchs and where sometimes hundreds can be seen at once. (Cape May is also a premier spot for the less celebrated dragonfly migration, including species such as globe trotters, green darners, saddlebags, and shadow dancers.)

There also are excellent West Coast butterfly-migration-watching locations. Natural Bridges State Beach near Santa Cruz, California, has a Monarch Trail in its eucalyptus grove; October through February are the best viewing months. And from late November through March in Santa Barbara, thousands of migrating monarchs alight on Pismo Beach's "butterfly trees" of eucalyptus and Monterey pine.

NEOTROPICAL SONGBIRD MIGRATIONS
Following the shore highway

Songbirds, much as monarch butterflies, make spectacular migrations that belie their diminutive sizes. In spring

migratory songbirds stream northward from the neotrop-
ics—hence the name. On the long migration, most songbirds maintain a modest speed of from thirty to forty miles
per hour. But to maintain energy reserves, most fly at night,
allowing them the opportunity to forage in daylight.

The flight between the Yucatán coast of Mexico and the
Gulf of Mexico shoreline of the United States is a challenging five to seven hundred miles. After reaching the North
American mainland, many songbirds follow the East and
West Coasts to northern nesting and feeding grounds. But
not all of them make it across the gulf. Once, an observer on
a ship thirty miles off the mouth of the Mississippi River
witnessed large numbers of migrating birds, mostly warblers, fly into a norther—a strong cold front with a brisk
northerly wind. Despite their already having completed
nine-tenths of the journey, most of them were unable to
contend and fell to their deaths.

Songbirds at sea will often alight to rest on ships, where
they provide a strange contrast to the ubiquitous gulls and
other seabirds. These impromptu visits often cheered up
weary sailors on long voyages because they speak of land
nearby. But on the Atlantic coast their presence anomalously
seaward usually means they were steered off course by a cold
air mass that bumped the tropical air mass they were flying
eastward in. Given this predicament, they will fall to sea exhausted, land on a ship, or touch down on an eastern-
extending landmass such as Cape Cod or Nova Scotia.

The spring migration can be grand, especially when
birds aggregate because of poor weather conditions. Dave
Taft, a park ranger friend of mine, was in awe of the bird life
around his preserve near New York Harbor early one May
1996 morning. A coastal storm had stalled to the south of
New York City and blocked the flyway for several days.

When the weather cleared, it was as if a dam had broken, releasing a torrent of frustrated warblers and other songbirds that alighted in droves after crossing lower New York Bay.

Indeed, timing these migrations during the meteorologically active seasons of spring and fall can be challenging for the little birds. Hay and Farb in *The Atlantic Shore* reported that insect-eating birds that advance northward too rapidly in spring may outdistance their food supply. When this occurs, their only hope for survival is to reverse direction and immediately fly southward, which may account for annual reports of "bewildered birds." They also told of how radar showed that during one night after a spring cold front had passed on Cape Cod, the northeasterly flight of birds was replaced by a milling movement, which was followed within two hours by a mass flight toward the south.

But sometimes making a living is uncomplicated; songbirds may experience the closest thing to a free lunch in marshes flooded by abnormally high tides. When this happens, insects hop, jump, and fly progressively onto the tallest plants until the grasses bend at the tips from the accumulations, making for easy pickings.

The fall migration of neotrops tends to be more dramatic, but there are many locations along the coast that deserve watching during either season. Because of its isolation in the Gulf of Maine, Monhegan Island is a magnet for tired, disoriented, and hungry migrant songbirds. During May and again from late August to mid-October the island may swarm with flickers, flycatchers, vireos, thrushes, warblers, and sparrows. Off the Rhode Island coast, Block Island's bayberry patches and reeds at times overflow with cuckoos, kinglets, and sparrows.

Numbers build in April and May, and then again in September and October, at Cape May, New Jersey. Ornithologist Joanna Burger described Cape May as "one of the world's great migration bottlenecks . . . the avian hub on the migration highway." The varied habitats, including an old dune forest at Higbee Beach in Cape May, make it an extremely popular birding spot from late August through October—at dawn the parking lot may be full already as early birders view some of the more than two hundred songbirds that have been sighted there. Average autumn days reveal about forty to fifty species, but there are poor days with few observed, and spectacular "fallout" days when a hundred kinds have been spotted (including as many as twenty-five warblers alone). Good locations farther southward include Cape Henlopen, Delaware; Assateague Island and Kiptopeke State Park, Virginia; and the Virginia National Wildlife Refuge (where birds tend to gather on the tip of the Eastern Shore before crossing the Chesapeake Bay) and Point Lookout, where the Potomac River meets the Chesapeake Bay.

On the Gulf of Mexico coast, Dauphin Island, Alabama, is an excellent spring birding area. Because the journey across the gulf is difficult, those that survive usually land on the first terra firma they find to eat, drink, and rest. Dauphin Island is one of best places on the Gulf Coast to experience these aerial fallouts.

The night migrations of songbirds are detectable, but conditions matter. On clear nights, especially when the moon shines brightly, migrating birds fly high, and the human ear can barely discriminate the faint twitterings. If clouds overspread, the flocks pass nearer to the earth and their notes are much more audible. And on very dark nights the flutter of their wings may be heard but a few feet overhead.

Many naturalists are concerned about neotropical songbirds because reliable counts demonstrate that populations are declining at a rapid rate. The future of these migrations is linked to the environmental health of the domains on both sides of the equator, with habitat loss—in both quantity and quality—being the main culprit.

❧❧❧

NOR'EASTERS

Winter's roundhouse punch

In *Notes from the Shore,* Jennifer Ackerman wrote that she tries to make a point of venturing out in all weathers, "even if only for a moment to feel the energies of the outside world." I especially love to walk the shore in a snowy nor'easter, when the sheer potency of the storm drains all color from the seascape, placid bays suddenly develop combers, and you must lean into the wind to make forward progress. You feel the cold of a winter nor'easter right to the bones. In fact, a collection of poems by Ruth Moore is called *Cold as a Dog and the Winds Northeast.*

But nor'easters (or, more correctly, no'theasters) do much more than chill. Large nor'easters whip the ocean into a fury. Winter gales can generate waves more than a thousand feet in length with speeds of more than seventy feet per second, or about forty-three knots. The frictional forces of sustained winds have a remarkable ability to pile up water. Although Europe does not sustain hurricanes, gales blowing in a constant direction lead to great storm surges, particularly in the North Sea, where they slide up the shores of England and the Low Countries. There they are called "sea bears" and they can be deadly—one sea bear that occurred in 1099 may have killed a hundred thousand people.

All nor'easters feature an arctic high-pressure system from the north and a subtropical low-pressure system from the south, with a front separating them. As the storm system starts spinning in a counterclockwise direction, a warm front to the east marks the leading edge of warm northbound air. As it rises over the colder, denser atmosphere to the north, the gently rising warm air generates steady rain or snow. Meanwhile, west of the storm's center, arctic air plunges south behind a cold front, along which heavier cold air wedges beneath the warm moist air. Forced upward, the warm air expands and cools, its moisture condensing and then precipitating. Once the system is formed, the earth's rotation causes the air to turn around its center. As incoming air rises around the core, the Jet Stream whisks it farther away, increasing the speed of the incoming air. The Jet Stream also tends to drag it along its usual winter path, northward along the coast.

When a large nor'easter approaches, air pressure drops; when it lowers more than twenty-four millibars in twenty-four hours, forecasters call it "The Bomb"—a big one is coming. The reduced air pressure also contributes to coastal flooding: A one-inch drop of barometric pressure allows the sea to rise more than thirteen inches. And what nor'easters don't achieve in wind speed compared to a hurricane, they make up for in duration with their sometimes slow progress and their size of up to a thousand miles in diameter.

The "Superstorm" of 1993, a gargantuan nor'easter, ranked third on *Weatherwise* magazine's list of the Twentieth Century's Top Ten U.S. Weather and Climate Events. Over March 12–15, this storm produced snowfall as widespread as any this century, with every major airport between Washington, D.C., and Boston shut down. Wind gusts on Long Island reached ninety-three miles per hour. As a Long Island resident, I was well aware of these blasts, especially when an eighty-five-foot tree near the curb fell across my lawn just after my children and I had left it following a romp in the snowdrifts. Although the storm was relatively well predicted, no one forecast the surge that killed residents of Florida's Big Bend coastline.

The details of nor'easters—how much rain and snow they'll drop and their exact path—are difficult to forecast, even with the technological tools of today. But one pattern is predictable: Big nor'easters are usually followed by strong nor'westers, which punch in cold dry air. A remarkable sequence of the two occurred in Maine during the severe storm of January 12, 1978. The nor'easter arrived not only at high tide, but on a celestial spring tide, causing water levels to rise ten feet higher than normal. The six-hour tempest was so intense that many coastal property owners couldn't recognize their lands or find their homes afterward. Just as the tide began to ebb, a cold front broke through and the abnormally high tide began to be driven out of the bays by sixty-knot winds. In these north–south trending bays, the water simply disappeared over minutes. A dinghy that was tied to a pier was, fifteen minutes later, hanging taut from its rope.

◈◈◈

OCEAN SUNFISH

Behold Mola mola

There is an oceangoing fish with a tall dorsal fin that stands high out of the water and frightens the uninitiated, who instantly think *shark*. But the ocean sunfish couldn't be less sharklike—it's a large, placid, odd-looking relative of the puffer that drifts the seas grazing jellyfish and seaweed.

The ocean sunfish is part of the *Mola*, or headfish, genus, so called because the animals appear to be little but head—just a great disc with eyes, a set of pectoral fins placed near the middle of its body, and dorsal and anal fins that jut

vertically; the rest of the animal appears to be missing. The fish also is armored by an incredibly thick skin of almost two inches and a layer of tough slime, and is often host to a large array of parasites. But despite its unlikely form and jellyfish diet, the mola can become huge, reaching eleven feet and weighing a ton.

Ocean sunfish often venture near ocean shores, where they alarm swimmers and mariners with their shark-suggestive fin. In cool northern waters they may be sluggish and even lie sideways. I've seen them just outside Long Island inlets, where they seem oblivious to nearby boat traffic. Once, a friend attempted to ride one, slipping into the water and managing to get his hands on the big dorsal fin. But the mola spooked, and with a great splash took off at a surprising speed for a fish that is all head.

OSPREYS

Fish hawks make a comeback

Spend time on an at least partly wild estuary or bay and there's a good chance you can spot an osprey, or fish hawk, scanning the waters. And if you're lucky, you may see it drop suddenly and, with exquisite timing, pluck a menhaden or other fish from the surface with its sharp talons. Sometimes the fish are surprisingly large; the osprey will have to work its wings hard to carry it aloft. Ospreys entertained Captain John Smith as he explored the Maine coast in the 1600s. Smith wrote: "Yet you shall see the wild hawks give pleasure in seeing them stoop six or seven after one another, at the schools of fish in the fair harbors."

Ospreys are superb fishers, with fish making up about 99 percent of their diets. They hunt from a height of about sixty feet, and when prey is spotted, they stall briefly and then plunge, turning feet-first before entering the water at speeds of twenty to forty miles an hour. On the way down they adjust their focus on the fish and correct their strike for light refraction, closing their nostrils with a flap of tissue. Ospreys fly with the fish facing forward after they lift it out of the water, presumably to reduce wind resistance. One scientist observed an osprey coming out of the water with two fish, one in each foot!

But ospreys also are capable of mistakes of judgment. One was seen being dragged under the surface of the St. Lucie River, Florida, by its intended victim. The bird eventually succeeded in freeing its talons, but was so nearly drowned that it lay on the deck of a yacht before recovering to fly. And once another osprey was seen being pulled underwater by a large fish it had seized; they were both found dead downriver a few days later, the fish still in the hawk's clutches.

Although bald eagles sometimes fish coastal waters, and may even chase ospreys to force them to yield their catches of fish, the osprey is the nearest regular presence to an eagle that much of the seaside has to offer. It is a truly cosmopolitan bird, occurring in every continent except Antarctica. It also is highly tolerant of people and a modicum of urbanization.

Because ponds and lakes heat faster than the sea, ospreys often feed in freshwater bodies in spring when they return from wintering in the Gulf of Mexico and southward, but they switch to the richer smorgasbord of marine waters as soon as these become warm enough for their fish prey to become active. In fact, it's estimated that 95 percent of their nests are constructed within sight of salt water.

Thirty years ago the future of this species in North America looked grim. The pesticide DDT—widespread in the environment and concentrated along the food chain—had reached high concentrations in the bodies of ospreys. Reproductive abnormalities resulted, including thin eggshells that were crushed when nesting ospreys sat on them.

But after DDT usage was banned in the early 1970s, ospreys began a remarkable comeback. Their return has been encouraged by wildlife managers and even classes of schoolchildren who have put up nesting platforms. Ospreys by nature prefer to nest in dead trees along the waterfront of their home ranges. But with development eradicating so much wild shorefront, and with decaying trees being taken down for safety and aesthetic reasons, areas that could otherwise support ospreys are limited by suitable nesting sites. In the nineteenth century coastal residents sometimes erected old wagon wheels on poles to use as nesting structures. Today, by placing simple squares of plywood on the top of eight- to twelve-foot-high posts to serve as platforms for their nests of sticks, we're allowing ospreys to continue their resurgence along much of the North American coastline. (But maybe they're too well adapted to man-made substitutes—they've even been found to use a piece of fishing net, shirts, a fertilizer bag, a rake, hula hoops, rag dolls, and toy boats as nesting materials; in the Chesapeake they've set up house on busted-up car bodies used as bombing targets and on an unexploded thousand-pound bomb.)

Nowadays, if you are anywhere along the North American coastline, you probably aren't far from an osprey. Areas of concentration include Shelter Island, Gardiners Island, and Long Island's north fork (where they often nest on telephone poles) in New York; Barnegat Bay, New Jersey; Cape Henlopen and Savage's Ditch, a marsh just north of the Indian River, Delaware; and all around the Chesapeake Bay, which may be home to one-quarter of the ospreys in the lower forty-eight states. In the Pacific Northwest look for them along large rivers.

PELICANS
Living cartoon characters

Pelicans are among the least likely of birds. Their most distinctive feature is that famous pouch that hangs from their lower jaws, ready to accommodate a feast's worth of fish. When they stand on a pier, mouth open, hoping an angler tosses them a fish, they resemble pterodactyls—the flying reptiles of dinosaur days. In fact, at those times fishermen may wish they were extinct because pelicans can become so brazen that they swallow hooked fish that are being reeled in, or they may go after fish that are in people's hands. It's not uncommon for pelicans that adopt fishing piers as their feeding grounds to have bills festooned with hooks and cutoff lines.

North America hosts two kinds of pelicans. The American white pelican has a pouch so large that it can hold four gallons of water. Like other birds, pelican parents regurgitate food to their hatchlings. But pelicans simply vomit into their own pouches, letting the young feed out of this dish. The white pelican was once found in the East but is now strictly a western coastal and inland dweller. Unlike the other seven pelican species found worldwide, the white doesn't plunge dive but instead in groups herds fish toward shore to scoop them up.

Brown pelicans are more marine than whites. Brown pelicans are found throughout the Gulf of Mexico and from Brazil to Cape Hatteras, but have recently been expanding their range. They often fly in single file. When a school of fish is spotted, a brown pelican folds its wings and from forty feet plummets with a great splash into the sea. But they can also swim and hop forward to engulf fish. The fish may wriggle in the loose pouch while excess water from the three and a half gallons taken in drains; then the bird points its bill skyward and lets the fish slide down its gullet. If it does this too slowly, a laughing gull may land on its head and snatch the fish away.

Although they have a reputation for competing for the same fish species humans prefer, in the Gulf of Mexico only 1 percent of the prey they take is edible to man. Most is a supremely oily herringlike fish called menhaden, which calorically for the bird is like living on Belgian chocolate. Whereas the lean codfish is composed of 1 percent total fat and the rich-tasting bluefin tuna is made up of about 5 percent, a menhaden is an astounding 20 percent fat.

As with the osprey, bald eagle, and other birds of prey, populations of brown pelicans plummeted as a result of chlorinated hydrocarbon pesticides, such as DDT and dieldrin. Historically, as many as eighty thousand individuals bred along the Louisiana coast; by 1961 there were no brown pelicans in the state that had chosen the pelican as its state bird! But as environmental conditions improved, they were reintroduced from Florida; Louisiana's population now numbers around thirty thousand.

Thousands of brown pelicans roost and nest on Sanibel Island on Florida's Gulf Coast and Pelican Island, in Indian River, on Florida's east coast. They have steadily been nesting farther north along the East Coast. Brown pelicans were rare in Virginia but since the 1980s have nested on Fisherman Island on the Eastern Shore. They reached the Chesapeake Bay in the late 1980s, choosing a hundred-foot stretch of little Shanks Island from the bay's nine thousand miles of shoreline. In the early 1990s young brown pelicans began building rudimentary nests in New Jersey's Barnegat Bay; ornithologists suspect this is a precursor to actual reproductive nesting. Lately, they've even been seen at inlets on the ocean side of Long Island, New York. On the West Coast the California brown pelican is found from Vancouver Island southward. They are often seen at Rodeo Beach just north of San Francisco and on the Farallon Islands, twenty miles offshore of the Golden Gate Bridge.

PFIESTERIA

The cell from hell

In the late 1980s great mortalities of fish covered with lesions and gaping holes began to occur in some mid-Atlantic estuaries. During 1991, in a fish kill in North Carolina's Neuse River that was blamed on *Pfiesteria*, nearly one billion fish died and bulldozers had to be brought in to clear the remains. *Pfiesteria* had struck, and hysteria was right behind.

Pfiesteria piscicida is a toxic dinoflagellate, a microscopic, free-swimming, single-celled organism discovered in 1988 by researchers at North Carolina State University. Since then, it's been learned that *Pfiesteria* has a highly complex life cycle, occurring in at least twenty-four forms. These include amoebas and nontoxic spores that can transform into toxic spores within minutes. But toxicity is related to the presence of fish waste products, not *Pfiesteria* cell numbers. Experiments have shown cell densities exceeding four hundred cells per milliliter of water to be toxic, while densities four times that without fish wastes were benign. When the *Pfiesteria* cells shift form and become activated, they begin to emit a powerful toxin that stuns fish, making them lethargic. Other toxins break down fish skin tissue, opening bleeding sores or lesions.

Fortunately, *Pfiesteria* outbreaks do not last for long. After such an event, *Pfiesteria* cells change back into nontoxic forms quickly, and the poisons in the water break down within a few hours. Still, once fish are weakened by the toxins, *Pfiesteria*-related lesions or fish kills may persist for days.

Pfiesteria piscicida is found from Mobile Bay, Alabama, northward to Delaware. But the greatest effects have been felt in North Carolina and, to a lesser extent, in the Chesapeake Bay. *Pfiesteria* appears to remain dormant until something triggers it, typically pollution in the form of nutrients. In North Carolina waste from hog farms is the major instigator.

But *Pfiesteria* doesn't just affect fish; it also causes serious health problems for people who come into contact with it. Watermen, divers, swimmers, and even researchers have had lesions and rashes on their bodies and have experienced irritableness and short-term memory loss—one angler was given a simple memory test of a list of ten items and could remember only three. And when in a research laboratory, aquarium aerators released the vapor into the air and a faulty ventilation system shunted it to a nearby office, it produced severe neurological symptoms in unsuspecting workers. So while hysteria is not warranted, a healthy respect for this new phenomenon is, including continuation of the fight against the overfertilization of inshore waters that brings out the worst in this strange microorganism.

PORTUGUESE MAN-OF-WARS

Sailboats with a sting

The Portuguese man-of-war is among the most dreaded animals of the sea. Anyone accidentally swimming into its tentacles will feel an immediate and excruciating pain of a searing, almost electriclike nature. Even slight contact can induce major discomfort that can last for hours and leave scars that remain for weeks. Once while pulling in the anchor line of a boat I was fishing on in the Florida Keys, my forearm touched a fragment of man-of-war tentacle that had caught on it as it drifted across; this slight contact left my arm incapacitated for the next hour. Severe stings while swimming can cause respiratory distress and muscular paralysis that can bring on drowning. So potent are its sting cells that even specimens found dried out high on a beach may inflict agony on a beachgoer's bare feet.

But despite its reputation as a creature to be avoided, a Portuguese man-of-war is also a magnificent being—one that is both surprisingly delicate for a menace and complicated for a watery invertebrate. Closely related to jellyfish, man-of-wars look like pink- and blue-hued cellophane bags on the sea. But these small floating structures support an array of tentacles that may reach more than 150 feet in length.

Portuguese man-of-wars are not the best sailors, despite their fancy "rigging" above the water's surface, but they can direct themselves to some extent. A deep-hulled sailboat can hold a course of almost forty-five degrees into the wind and is blown sideways only about five degrees. In contrast, a man-of-war sails at about 145 degrees to the wind and it loses 95 degrees—about what you could manage in a washtub with a sheet on a stick.

Man-of-wars are lopsided—the budding of submerged body parts off their floats are asymmetrical, producing either "right-" or "left-handed" specimens. It once was thought that this was related to whether individuals lived in the Northern or Southern Hemispheres, a notion that was abandoned when both kinds were found in the Canary Islands. (It's also true that a sampling of both kinds would be biased according to prevailing wind conditions.)

The Portuguese man-of-war is common from Florida to Texas and along the east coast of Florida. Occasionally they are driven ashore by storms from the Gulf Stream to Cape Hatteras, and sometimes as far north as Cape Cod, but such events are rare—it was considered noteworthy when seven washed ashore on a beach in eastern Long Island, New York, in 1984.

PUFFERS

Fish with a comical defense mechanism

There is a fish that performs a simple trick that impresses adults and mesmerizes children—the puffer or "blowfish." The puffer is a slow-moving, inshore creature that might easily fall prey to larger fish. But it has a unique defense, readily exhibited when captured. When other fish are caught, the show is over. But cradle a puffer in your hands and stroke its bottom and it huffs and gulps air, filling the special sac in its belly and becoming almost spherical and three times larger—an almost impossible object to swallow, and made even more difficult by a sandpapery hide. An inflated fish thrown back in the water will float on its back for a while before it exhales.

While in the sea, they achieve the same swelled effect by filling with water. And this defense works; recently, a forty-pound striped bass was pulled by hand out of the surf at Long Island, New York, the great fish near death with an inflated puffer in its throat, gamely refusing to be swallowed. Puffers have also been seen being carried off by birds of prey, only to slip the talons' grasp by becoming too round to grip.

Puffers are surprisingly effective predators themselves, capable of taking apart a healthy blue crab—which as any crabber knows is a formidable opponent. A gang of puffers will surround the crustacean, with a few engaging the crab from the front while others rush in from behind and clip off its legs, after which they all rush in and share in the feast.

The northern puffer commonly found on the East Coast reaches about a foot in length; in summer it ranges in catchable numbers to New York, but is sometimes seen as far north as Maine. It is a species of an essentially tropical family that includes better-armed members such as the porcupine fish, which wards off predators with both a bloated belly and quill-like spines. Porcupine fish are sometimes dried out whole and sold for display as "Japanese lanterns."

PUFFINS

Sea parrots

The puffin, or sea parrot, is the nearest thing to a penguin the Northern Hemisphere has to offer. Puffins are not related to the Antarctic penguins, but there is a degree of evolutionary convergence between them—they've evolved a similar tuxedo-clad look while occupying a parallel ecological niche. And they are endearing. Thorndike wrote, "The puffin is one of nature's playful inspirations, like the dolphin and panda, that arouse a response of instant delight."

The puffin is a bird of cold northern places, from most of Greenland south to Maine. When lined up on a rocky coastal ledge, puffins are a striking sight, with their black-and-white bodies, red legs, white faces, and triangular bills in brilliant red and yellow lending them a clownlike look. But when this stocky bird enters the water, it becomes a most efficient predator of fish. It swims and dives skillfully, and because the edges of its bill have sharp serrations, a puffin can hold many fish at once crosswise—someone once counted twenty-eight.

Puffins, like so many colonial seabirds, suffered great losses at the hand of humans. But none so much as its relative the great auk, a three-foot-tall penguinlike bird that was the nuclear submarine of the world's diving birds—great auks hunted in packs down to depths of forty fathoms as they pursued schools of herring, smelt, and capelin. But they were both flightless and without guile—easy prey that was hunted ruthlessly. Jacques Cartier wrote of the great auk of Funk Island off Nova Scotia, which he called the Island of Birds, "... whereof there is such plenty that unless a man did see them, we would think it an incredible thing ... they seemed to have been brought thither and sowed for the nonce. In less than two hours we filled two boats full of them as if they had been stones." An island colony off Labrador of about half a million great auks was virtually wiped out in a season. Today no man can see them: The great auk was driven to extinction in 1844.

Because of concentrated hunting of colonial seabirds for meat, feathers, and eggs, their populations in North Atlantic waters declined. One colonist wrote, "There is nothing that swims the water, flies the air, crawls or walks the earth that I have not served upon my table." In his case this included boiled owls and roasted crows. To cook puffins, the carcass was slit down the back, opened flat like a kipper, then propped upright on the hearth and grilled in front of the fire. When in 1832 John James Audubon traveled to Maine to sketch and paint them, he reported, "Birds are very, very few and far between." He returned the next year and had a difficult time finding even gulls! Audubon had to journey all the way to Labrador to find specimens to draw. Fortunately, with the notably sad exception of the great auk, North Atlantic seabird numbers rebounded and can easily be viewed today.

Puffins have an unusual breeding characteristic that complicates population recovery efforts, however. They nest in burrows on rocky islands and return to the same ones each year. But they home so effectively that when an island's population for some reason becomes extinct, they don't readily recolonize new ones. Since 1907 U.S. colonies had been reduced to those on two remote Maine islets—Matinicus Rock and Machias Seal Island. To increase the number of puffin colonies, in 1974 biologists moved fifty-four eight-day-old puffin chicks from Newfoundland to burrows on Eastern Egg Rock—a suitable but uncolonized island in Maine's Muscongus Bay (said to have the greatest number of lobster buoys anywhere)—with the hope that they would return as adults five years later, and this strategy was repeated in subsequent years.

The chicks were stuffed full of fish and then abandoned after a time so they would venture into the sea and fend for themselves. It took just a little longer than half a decade—the first returnees showed in 1981. As the program grew, more persuasion was used to coax them back—the biologists placed puffin dummies and played taped seabird calls to convince them. As of 2001, the colony had thirty-seven nesting pairs and twenty-five younger birds not ready to breed.

Puffins can sometimes be seen from ferries that leave from Maine or Nova Scotia and the rest of the Canadian Maritimes. Machias Seal Island, nine miles off the Maine coast, is a prime nesting spot for puffins in June and July. Puffin-watching cruises are available from Jonesport and Cutler. And the Pacific coast has its own puffin, an even sillier-looking tufted kind, that is found on offshore islands from Alaska to Santa Barbara, California.

∽∾∾

"RED SKY IN MORNING, SAILORS TAKE WARNING" AND OTHER SEA WEATHER INDICATORS

The wise mariner watches for weather signs

"Red sky in morning, sailors take warning" is nautical advice so familiar that even the most fervent landlubbers know it. But in every corner of our coasts mariners have observed particular weather patterns that tell of storms or winds of potentially major consequences. Henry Beston in *The Outermost House* wrote about how in Cape Cod, "There comes no good of the western wind when it backs against the sun." Wyman Richardson, also writing about Cape Cod, had long noted that a breeze that hung to the southeast of his house on Cape Cod, and freshened in late afternoon or after sunset, boded ill; indeed, it preceded the infamous 1938 hurricane.

Visual cues to maritime weather abound for those who know how to interpret them. "Sun dogs," hazy spots located to each side of the sun in an afternoon lightly overcast, announce deteriorating weather and rain for the following day. Cloud sequences announce coming storms, with increasing and lowering banks generally indicative of soon worsening conditions. But the keen observer can note rain on its way as much as about two days early by watching for wispy "mare's tails" and a "mackerel sky" of high wavy-patterned clouds, which signal the leading edge of a warm front. This sparked a rhyme worth remembering: "Mare's tails and mackerel scales make tall ships take in their sails."

Rainbows form as light is refracted through raindrops that act as tiny prisms; they can only be seen with our backs against the sun. Looking west at a morning rainbow suggests rain for later in the day as moisture-laden air moves eastward; an oppositely arcing evening rainbow is a sign of a clear night and sunny tomorrow as damp air moves away. And unlike the red-sky-in-morning warning, a fiery sunset means clear sailing. For those who remember rhymes better than mere facts, there is of course a rainbow ditty: "Rainbow windward, foul falls the day. Rainbow leeward, damp runs away."

Approaching storms also announce their impending arrival with swells that precede them. Long, high waves rolling in tell us that powerful winds have been at work some distance away, and the longer the swells, the more potent the storm. Increasingly large swells indicate the storm is approaching; this cue may occur even before the sky shows additional evidence. This happens most dramatically before a hurricane—large waves and a pounding surf may be experienced on the New Jersey coast from a hurricane centered in the West Indies.

Thoreau, in *Cape Cod*, told the story of a particularly astute observer of a subtle but reliable hurricane sign. On a journey to the West Indies, an old man familiar with the region announced upon sounding the depth that they should make certain preparations to head immediately at full speed to the island destination. It seems he had seen the lead in the water at a distance of many fathoms more than he had seen it before, that the water was clear all of a sudden, and that this was a sign of an impending hurricane at sea. They made it to shore by rowboat before the height of the storm, and their own ship was tossed so far inland that several weeks elapsed before it could be launched.

The mariner's weather eye can be considerably aided by a simple tool, the barometer, which measures air pressure and thus is sensitive to the all-important interplay between high- and low-pressure systems. A "wind-barometer" table, combined with knowledge of wind direction, is a useful local-weather forecaster. A southwest-to-northwest shift and barometer readings of 30.10 to 30.20 "inches of mercury" and steady foretell fair conditions, with slight temperature changes for one or two days. But beware a south-to-east wind shift with a barometer reading of 29.80 and falling rapidly—a severe storm is imminent.

RED TIDES

Beware of colored waters

The Red Sea received its name from long-ago mariners who saw the reflections of its mineral-rich reddish hillsides. Waters that actually are red, however, may be colorful, but they're not healthy and can even be dangerous. The term *red tides* is given to a number of phenomena. Most red tides are caused by dinoflagellates, which are so small that it takes twenty-five thousand of them to measure an inch.

Although many species cause red tides, only a few are fatal to other organisms. Some are only bothersome. In September 1999 a plume of red algae at Robert Moses State Park in New York forced the park administrators to keep the twenty-nine thousand visitors out of the water; many left the sands early because of the algal bloom's stench. A green algal bloom had closed a nearby beach a few weeks earlier. But the blooms to be seriously concerned with are those that release powerful neurotoxins. The low-oxygen conditions that occur during these blooms may also contribute to the deaths of sea creatures. And sometimes a red tide "gas" is associated with blooms; the aerosol comes from the mechanical breakdown of the dinoflagellates, the toxin being carried in the wind in a finely suspended mist. Waves, wind, and the churn of boat propellers contribute to its spread. Unsuspecting residents of afflicted areas sometimes believe that nerve gas has been released. Eyes and noses burn and dry, lips tingle, and a choking cough ensues.

Florida red tide blooms typically begin offshore in the Gulf of Mexico and move southeast toward the Tampa Bay region. Surprisingly, these blooms have recently been tied to events in Africa: Clouds of dust from the Sahara may fall on the gulf and deposit enough iron—a nutrient typically in short supply in the sea—to launch a bloom. The devastation caused by red tides on Florida's southwest coast has been well chronicled. In the most severe episode ever observed, lasting from November 1946 to September the following year, resort beaches were covered with dead fish. The 1963 red tide in Tampa Bay brought to shore more than 150 tons of fish, including a seven-hundred-pound grouper. A bloom in 1964 north of Tarpon Springs covered fourteen thousand square miles.

When a red tide bloom is severe, fish die quickly from the neurotoxic effects, so the poison doesn't build up in their tissues. But when fish are exposed to lower concentrations, they may accumulate these toxins. When higher-ups in the food chain eat these fish, the poison dose may be fatal. This phenomenon may have been why more than seven hundred dolphins perished in 1987. Red tides have also killed many manatees, bringing about a pneumonialike respiratory distress.

Red tides, like other microbial blooms, seem to be fertilized by certain naturally occurring chemicals in the water. But warm weather, low salinities, and calm conditions may hasten red tide development. Also, red tides are not always red—they may be yellow, pink, green, blue, black, purple, or brown, and a bloom from a single species may change colors depending on its life stage. General guidelines are that it's safe to eat crabs, lobsters, shrimp, and fish from red tide waters, but not bivalves such as oysters and clams.

Far from the Gulf of Mexico, in the Canadian Maritimes, dwell other red-tide-causing microorganisms, but they're algae instead of dinoflagellates. These algae also bloom furiously, with a single cell replicating itself as much as one million times in two to three weeks. These algae give off domoic acid, which is potentially lethal, and what seem like tiny amounts sometimes kill humans.

But the northern form of red tides actually comes in three varieties, all of which produce severe and unique symptoms. *Alexandrium* causes paralytic shellfish poisoning for which there is no antidote; death occurs from asphyxiation or respiratory paralysis. Diarrhetic shellfish poisoning is caused by *Dinopysis*. Extreme gastrointestinal distress occurs, which may lead to death from dehydration or other complications. *Pseudo-nitzchia multiseries* induces amnesiac shellfish poisoning, which begins with stomach upset, followed by dizziness, disorientation, and memory loss, and occasionally death from brain damage.

A diary from 1793 tells of the voyagers of the *Discovery* who found some mussels along the Nova Scotia shore and boiled and ate a quantity of them. Those who ate the mussels were soon stricken with numbness about the mouth, face, and arms, which soon spread over the whole body, "accompanied with giddiness and general lassitude. . . ." One of the crew members vomited but then felt well enough to help row the tender. But then he fell down and had to be brought to shore, where a fire was prepared to boil water as an emetic. Before the water was ready, his pulse weakened, his mouth and lips turned black, and his face and neck became swollen, together with faintness, general numbness, and tremor. He expired within five hours of eating the contaminated mussels.

Other kinds of dangerous red tides are found throughout much of the world, including a dinoflagellate, *Gonyaulax*, along the West Coast. Because microbial blooms are associated with warm weather, they may be responsible for the old admonition to eat oysters only during months that have the letter *r* in them. But there are other folklorish ways to monitor the safety of seafood. The Abenaki Indians avoided paralytic shellfish poisoning by going out the night before they planned to harvest shellfish and stirring the water over the beds. They had learned that if the water revealed a certain phosphorescent glow from bioluminescent plankton, they should move on to another bay. Maine waterfowlers use their own approach. So long as the sea ducks they shoot have mussels and other bivalves in their crops, the shellfish are safe to eat. But if the ducks switch to baby crabs and other non-water-filtering invertebrates, the shellfish are to be avoided.

REVERSING FALLS
Ping-Pong waters

Near Saint John in New Brunswick there is a narrow tidal strait with a flow so wild and forceful that kayakers rate it above the famed Colorado and Honduras Rivers. And unlike true rivers, the currents in this tortured artery change direction every twelve hours: thus its name, Reversing Falls.

Samuel de Champlain encountered these falls on a voyage in 1604, recounting: "The river is dangerous, if one does not observe carefully certain points and rocks on the two sides. It is narrow at the entrance, and then becomes broader. A certain point is passed, it becomes narrower again, and forms a kind of fall between two large cliffs, where the water runs so rapidly that a piece of wood thrown in is drawn under and not seen again. But by waiting till high tide you can pass this fall easily."

How can a passage go from maelstrom to placid strait? The phenomenon of the Reversing Falls is caused by an interaction between the Saint John River and the world's highest tides in the Bay of Fundy, which reach twenty-eight and a half feet near Saint John. At low tide in Saint John Bay, waters from the Saint John River flow inward through a narrow gorge. An underwater ledge thirty-six feet below the surface causes the water to tumble downward into a two-hundred-foot-deep pool, after which it boils in a series of rapids and whirlpools.

But as the sea begins to rise on the flooding tide, it slows the course of the river and finally stops its flow completely. This short period of slack tide is the only time that boats can navigate the falls. Then the tides rise farther, and slowly the flow reverses and heads upstream. As the rise continues the rapids begin to re-form, but now in the opposite direction. At full high tide the tidal waters are more than fourteen feet higher than the river. The process then reverses again, until the tidal waters reach a point about fourteen feet lower than river level.

Reversing Falls often has members of an elite cadre of kayakers practicing on it—everyone else should do no more than watch. Whereas a typical white-water river moves less than ten thousand cubic feet of water per second—sometimes a good deal less—the flow at Reversing Falls thunders through at more than ten times that. To best appreciate Reversing Falls, they should be viewed at least twice on a given day: once near high tide and once near low, about twelve hours apart. There is a good vantage point in aptly named Fallsview Park, near the Reversing Falls Information Center.

Similar but smaller-scale versions of this phenomenon exist, such as Cobscook Reversing Falls under the Roosevelt Memorial International Bridge near Lubec, New Brunswick. The Pacific coast has its own celebrated reversing waters: Butze Rapids near Prince Rupert in British Columbia. The turbulence there is most dramatic about half an hour after high tide.

ॐ

SAINT ELMO'S FIRE

Supernatural candles

In *Moby-Dick* the appearance in a lightning storm of burning spires on the tips of the *Pequod*'s masts and yardarms transfixed the frightened crew and was seen by Ahab as the white flame that lit the way to the White Whale. This manifestation—Saint Elmo's fire—is one of the eeriest and most evocative phenomena the sea can offer.

Saint Elmo's fire's flamelike appearance is typically seen during stormy or threatening weather on the high points of sailing ships. It is usually bluish or greenish in color, but sometimes violet or white. The fire is hardly visible in daylight, but day or night the light is usually accompanied by a sizzling or crackling noise.

Henry Wadsworth Longfellow summarized the meteorological significance of Saint Elmo's fire in his poem "Golden Legend."

Last night I saw Saint Elmo's stars,
With their glittering lanterns all at play
On the tops the masts and the tips of the spars,
And I knew we should have foul weather today.

Records of the phenomenon of Saint Elmo's fire extend far back in history. It is named for Saint Ermo—the patron saint of Mediterranean sailors—whose name was subsequently corrupted to Elmo. Given its ethereal nature, it's not surprising that it was also known as *corposant* (holy body) by Mediterranean sailors, who believed it to be a visitation by the actual guardian come to warn them.

The ancient Greeks considered it a sign that their ship was under the protection of Castor and Pollux, the guardians of sailors. It has shown up elsewhere than the rigging of ships. Pliny the Elder's *Natural History* states that it sometimes appeared on men's heads. And a description of a storm in Julius Caesar's *Commentaries* includes this: ". . . and the same night the points of spears belonging to the Fifth Legion seemed to take fire."

Some displays of Saint Elmo's fire have been particularly striking. In March 1866 the fire appeared in stormy weather on an iron ship sailing in the English Channel. The captain saw blades of light on the top of the mainmast and at the tips of the yardarms, with a most vivid spire of light emerging from the bowsprit. Climbing to the bowsprit where the light shot up into space, he approached his hand to the "flame." Although it radiated no appreciable heat, the fire then emerged from his fingertips! Furthermore, the entire array of lights around the ship faithfully followed the variations of the squall; each time the wind increased and the rain fell harder, the splendor grew greater.

Saint Elmo's fire actually is a weak to moderately intense electrical discharge from the atmosphere that is more or less continuous for a time. Emanating from elevated objects at the earth's surface or ships, the discharge occurs when the electrical field in the neighborhood of the object becomes very strong, as when a thundercloud is in the vicinity. The visible discharge consists of innumerable tiny sparks. Each produces a tiny "explosion" of the air through which it passes, resulting in a sizzling or hissing sound not usually audible from more than a few feet away. But the sparks may grow larger and louder and end in, or with, a flash of lightning.

There is much about atmospheric electricity that remains mysterious; it's better to retreat to safety when sensed. Anglers should be especially aware, because often the fishing peaks during a storm. Two fellows were once casting for bass, fully aware that a thunderstorm was bearing down on them but stalling their departure because the fish were striking with abandon. But when they happened to cast at the same time and both of their lines remained suspended in the air by some electrical force instead of settling to the water, their eyes widened with amazement. They gunned the engine and were gone in a flash, pun intended.

❧

SAND STRANDS AND OTHER KINDS OF BEACHES

It's not always soft and brown

As a beach bum whose old Volkswagen camper got stuck more than once in the soft sand at Montauk, New York, I was awfully surprised to see locals driving their everyday sedans right up to the surf line at Daytona Beach in Florida. Coarse sands don't pack well and so are difficult to walk on; fine sands pack more closely, supporting feet or automobile tires. Whereas in most places making even slow progress on beaches with vehicles requires four-wheel drives and partially deflated tires, in some spots such as Daytona the particular qualities of the sands allows them to compact to form surfaces almost as firm as your asphalt driveway. Sands that can be easily driven on are also found in California at Pismo Beach and in Washington near the mouth of the Columbia River.

Beaches are not strictly made of sands—the shores of Labrador may be lined with heavy cobbles, and various grades of rock below that occur all around North America, from flat "shingle" rocks, through gravel, to fine, dusty powders. The cobblestones and pebbles are not endpoints, although they may seem so across a human's existence—both will be reduced further over geological time to sand particles. But on reaching a certain degree of fineness, the process halts as each tiny grain is shielded from erosive contact with other grains by a film of water around them.

The gradations of particle size have ramifications. The angle of a shore normally reflects the heft of the components that make up a beach: A cobble beach may slope at almost twenty degrees, a shingle or gravel beach at twelve degrees, and a calcareous sand beach may have an almost imperceptible incline. Beaches also may or may not be well sorted—that is, made up of the same-sized particles. Particle size and uniformity are easily assessed—just pick some up and run it between your fingers. And if you go to the trouble of looking at a random grab of sand under a microscope, you will see a granular world of varying and sometimes brilliant color.

The sands of beaches reflect the sources of material. Along much of the Atlantic and Gulf of Mexico coasts, the particles were created long ago by glacial rivers and carried to the sea, then distributed by currents and winds. The sands of the Bay of Fundy are largely reddish, echoing their sandstone origins. Rachel Carson wrote, "Every grain of sand on a New England beach has a long and eventful history. Before it was sand, it was rock—splintered by the chisels of the frost, crushed under advancing glaciers and carried forward with the ice in its slow advance, then ground and polished in the mill of the surf."

Much of the U.S. Atlantic coast is made up of light-colored granitic sands of quartz and feldspar. The "sandy beach" at Acadia National Park in Maine is about 60 percent quartz granules; the remainder is mostly shell and urchin-spine fragments, giving the sand a sawdustlike texture. Jasper Beach in Machiasport, Maine, is made up of ultrasmooth jasper stones in red, green, brown, and yellow. West Quoddy Head in Maine, the easternmost point in the United States, has black volcanic sands under its up-to-two-hundred-foot cliffs.

Lovely blackish red garnet sands are common on Long Island, where they accumulate in thin drifts over lighter-colored sands. The pinkish sands of Popham Beach, Maine, have a high percentage of garnet. Sands from Massachusetts to northern Florida are similar in makeup, but with higher proportions southward of calcium carbonate from shell fragments: less than 0.5 percent north of Virginia, about 5 percent immediately south of it, and as much as 10 percent between Cape Hatteras and Cape Lookout in North Carolina.

In southern Florida the white calcite beaches are primarily organic in origin, composed of fragments of coral, shells, and sea urchin spines. The weight-resistant beach at Daytona is made up of hard-packing quartz granules. In Venice, Florida, the sand has a special glitter from crystals of zircon dusted over its surface. The sand of Florida's shell-littered Sanibel Island is almost completely made up of shell particles, so finely ground that it clings to feet like dust. But the not-faraway Florida panhandle beaches are almost all quartz sands eroded from mountains hundreds of miles away in Georgia. Sand on west Florida's undersea continental shelf is twelve thousand feet deep in places; elsewhere it is only inches deep over hard limestone.

Certain beaches are made up of egg-shaped "cabochons," well-rounded pieces of quartz, feldspars, gneisses, granites, graphites, sandstones, and conglomerates. Some sands have dark iron granules—run a magnet through them and you'll pick up ilmenite and magnetite. Other dark particles may be garnets that glisten in deep red when examined under a microscope. Sands may also contain grains of amethyst, tourmaline, topaz, and sapphire.

On the West Coast, San Diego's Del Mar Beach is made up largely of soft green limestone shingles, whereas northern California's rugged "Lost Coast" has black sand beaches. Because of a seasonal reversal of wind and wave direction, sand is transported to the northern ends of beaches in winter and to the southern ends in summer.

Some sands near urban areas show a strong human influence, with much broken glass and pottery contributing to the mix. Particular beaches in New York Harbor are reddish not from sandstone but because they are composed almost completely of coal clinkers left behind from industrial use.

Sand beaches are constantly mutating; Rachel Carson wrote that "For no successive days is the shoreline precisely the same." The ever-evolving patterns made by the meeting of sand and sea, under the direction of currents and wind, are best observed as a clean slate early in the morning before humans have disturbed them, especially on a low tide when more of the beach is revealed. Drifts, domes, scarps, holes, funnels, and fields of ripples form an ephemeral, but always enchanting topography.

On a larger scale, storms and littoral drift open and close the inlets through sand beaches across the ages. There are good records of the principal inlets on the Outer Banks since the late 1500s. Just a small minority are open today, and most of these didn't form until the mid-1880s to the 1930s; only Ocracoke Inlet spans both today and 1585, when the existence of these inlets were first recorded. Many other inlets had lives of only a few years or decades.

But the same mobility of sands that creates renewing terrains also denudes beaches and evaporates islands. It once wiped out a community in coastal Oregon, too. In 1907 a Kansas City developer named T. B. Potter planted the "Queen of Oregon Resorts" on a sandy spit and called it Bayocean. The town soon had a hotel, grocery, bowling alley, and the largest indoor saltwater swimming pool on the West Coast. But in 1917 construction of Tillamook Bay's north jetty changed coastal currents, and street after street began washing into the sea. A 1932 jetty extension hastened the process. By 1952 the spit was an island and the city but a memory.

SAND EELS

Fish moles

There is a small, slender, superficially eel-like fish that can disappear before your eyes. When threatened, sand eels (aka sand launces) can bury into the sand for protection to a depth of six inches. More amazingly, they may spend time in the sand above the waterline. Sometimes they startle clam diggers; one account included seeing "a great section of the beach" in Provincetown Harbor become "alive with dancing forms of dozens of these agile fishes."

Sand eels are mysterious in their sudden appearances, and it's not clear whether they come and go or simply remain buried in the sand for extended periods. They are pursued by a great number of predators, including porpoises, which have been seen rooting them out of the bottom. But the sand eels' noses are so sharp that when they are swallowed by cod, and perhaps other fish, they sometimes work right through the stomachs and into the body cavities of their captors, to become encysted in the body wall.

Other dedicated pursuers are terns, which are expert hunters of sand eels. They hover and watch, and then dive headfirst to emerge with a wriggling sand eel in their beaks—a feat of amazing precision and dexterity. Equally impressive is the bird's ability to almost bounce back out of an underwater dive to immediately become airborne and ready to fish again.

Sand eels are found from Cape Hatteras north to the Canadian Maritimes. A common way of gathering them is to score wet sand below the high-tide mark with a specially designed rake. But more intriguing is the typical English method, using a "vingler." A vingler is simply a long, narrow, but dull knife. Drag the blade through likely wet sand spots, feeling for resistance. When a sand eel is felt, the expert swings the vingler upward and grabs the emergent sand eel before it falls back on the sand, where it would instantly disappear. But there is some risk involved—British beaches are also home to burrowing weever fish that bear poisonous spines. Still, good vingler wielders can sense the difference in resistance and halt their motion before they squeeze a weever.

∽∽∽

SARGASSUM WEED AND
GULF STREAM WASHUP

Gifts from our offshore river

Way out in the Atlantic Ocean, a little north of the equator, lies a vast, largely becalmed two-million-square-mile region called the Sargasso Sea. This nutrient-poor reach has little microscopic algae in it to cloud its waters, and so it is crystal clear. But floating on its surface are mats of sargassum weed or gulfweed, a brown leafy alga with pea-sized floats that may live for tens of years to centuries. From an airplane, viewers may see neatly aligned rows of sargassum as golden streamers against the midnight blue of deep tropical ocean. These patterns reflect local circulation that accumulates the weed in amounts as great as five and a half tons per square mile. At times winds concentrate sargassum in giant rafts so dense that legends developed of ships being engulfed and immobilized.

The jungles of sargassum support its own unique ecology. In fact, 10 percent of the animals found in the sargassum weed community are found nowhere else. The associated fauna includes sea turtles, crabs, barnacles, and fan worms. There's even a six-inch-long fish that has evolved to look just like a stringy ball of sargassum weed called, appropriately enough, the sargassumfish.

Sargassum weed may become entrained in the circulation system that brushes the Sargasso Sea. This includes, in the Gulf of Mexico, the Gulf Loop current—a river of warm tropical water several hundred miles across and two thousand feet deep that churns in a great clockwise gyre. Sometimes this current captures fifty-mile-wide eddies of Mississippi River outflow and carries these parcels around the south tip of Florida at Key West; satellite photos have shown them reaching the coast of Georgia before mixing and losing their identity.

When the loop current rounds Florida it's called the Gulf Stream, a rushing current that rings the North Atlantic and is critical in the transfer of heat from the Tropics to higher latitudes. So distinct is this ribbon of water that it rides about one foot higher than the surrounding sea. It was first mapped at the insistence of then–postmaster general Benjamin Franklin, who learned of it from a Nantucket skipper. Franklin used it to speed mail delivery to Europe; for a time Englishmen resisted being counseled by "simple American fishermen" and continued to buck the current coming west, which prolonged their voyages by two weeks. American whalers had recorded its path because they had learned that whales never occupied its food-poor waters.

Later, the Gulf Stream becomes broad and sluggish after reaching Europe, where it is called the Canaries Current. It then crosses westward from Africa as the Equatorial Current; part of this flow pushes into the Gulf of Mexico as the Yucatán Current off the Straits of Yucatán, and then becomes the Gulf Loop.

This oceanwide conveyor belt picks up and moves around many organisms. Giant whirlpools of the loop current sometimes break off and move along the coast, dispersing sea anemones and butterfly fish to Panama City, Florida, and floating purple oceanic snails to Port Aransas, Texas. Upwellings may bring deep-water octopuses and luminescent lantern fish ashore together with sargassum weed. When thickets of sargassum drift closer to the mainland, they may attract huge numbers of juvenile fish. One researcher sorted through three and a half tons of it taken from the Florida Current southeast of Key Biscayne and found eighty-four hundred individual young fish of fifty-four species. North winds sometimes bunch up sargassum weed offshore, creating weed lines that anglers seek because the gathering baitfish also attract gamefish such as sailfish, dolphinfish, and cobia.

Sometimes strong winds blow sargassum weed clumps or rafts right onto the beach. This is a great opportunity to see up close life that normally resides in the deep ocean hundreds of miles from shore. Sift through it carefully, preferably with a small dip net, and you may discover some exotic creatures. Areas that are known for stranded sargassum weed include the Gulf of Mexico shore and, along the East Coast, Cape Hatteras and Martha's Vineyard and Nantucket—locations that are nearest the Gulf Stream. But persistent winds may drive the weed shoreward anywhere along the East Coast south of Cape Cod.

࿇

SEA BEANS
Wandering fruits

Rivers carry vast amounts of plant material into the sea, including seeds. Most seeds are ill suited to survive in seawater, but "sea beans" are world travelers. True sea beans are from the Tropics and drift north on the Gulf Stream. Because sea beans are so buoyant, they are often found stranded at the highest storm drift lines. Few make it to shore north of Cape Hatteras. But many are carried to Great Britain and other parts of Europe.

Sea beans were believed to have curative value and even occult powers in Europe, where they were exotic—midwives carried such stones as part of their equipment. The dark, kidney-shaped *Entada* bean was thought to serve functions that were contradictory: In Ireland they were eaten in the hope of increasing fertility, whereas in Australia they were valued as an oral contraceptive. They also were fashioned into snuff boxes, bottles, teething rings, and amulets. The presence of sea beans in Europe was said to have inspired Christopher Columbus to search for undiscovered lands to the west.

The best-known seaborne fruit is, of course, the coconut. The coconut is among the most useful plant products on earth, having been used as a source of food, drink, cooking oil, fuel, vinegar, and fibers for making rope.

Beaches near river mouths often have walnuts, acorns, and hickory nuts, which may remain viable for a short time. For journeys of many years, seedpods must have high survival characteristics, including a tough coating and the ability to capitalize on felicitous strandings. Mango seeds remain buoyant up to three months, long enough to be carried by the Gulf Stream from the Florida Keys and Bahamas to the New York Bight. Long seedlings of red mangroves float all over the world in warm waters and quickly put down roots where the climate is right. The tree is well adapted to shifting substrates—even two-inch-tall seedlings have root systems that are nearly impossible to pull out by hand.

A sea bean that rides Pacific currents is the country almond fruit, a peachlike pod with an outer skin, fleshy interior, and almondlike stone. Native to Hawaii, this seed has been found in Oregon after a trip on the Kuroshio Current of 11,100 miles and seven years.

SEALS AND SEA LIONS
Watch for bobbing heads

Seals and sea lions are among the more endearing of sea creatures. One theory as to why is that their eyes are captivating: large, brown liquid pools with almost no irises. The seals or pinnipeds come in two main varieties, the "earless" or "true seals" that have no visible external ear, and the "eared," which include fur seals and sea lions. The rear flippers of true seals are fused as a single tail, which is cumbersome on land, whereas fur seals and sea lions have separate rotatable rear flippers that allow them high mobility on beaches.

The most likely seal to be seen along much of North America's Atlantic coast is the harbor seal. Harbor seals are inshore pinnipeds that coexist well with humans. They are also highly intelligent, capable of recognizing individual boats from which people have shot at them in the past. Maine alone may host five to six thousand harbor seals. And they appear to be becoming more numerous southward along the mid-Atlantic as their populations build. A harbor seal that hauled out and sunned itself every day on a floating dock created a local sensation for three weeks in January 1989 in Shark River Inlet, New Jersey. Today, from November through May, more than four thousand seals can be found from Long Island's Montauk Point to New York City, a tenfold increase in fifteen years. Recently, they began to winter on some man-made islands in lower New York Harbor that are within sight of Manhattan. But the farther north you go, the more routinely seals of several species, including gray and hooded seals, may be seen. Seals are found all summer long at the eastern tip of the Gaspé Peninsula at Forillon National Park.

Although many associate seals with cold waters, there are species of monk seal found throughout the Mediterranean Sea and around the Hawaiian Islands. Until the last century the Caribbean monk seal was found from south Florida to the Bahamas, Jamaica, Mexico, and Central America. Despite the reputation of their meat as being especially unpalatable, colonies of these seals were easy prey for hungry European explorers and colonists beginning with Christopher Columbus, who killed eight "sea wolves" he found on a rocky island near Haiti. The final member of the last colony—at Seranilla Bank between Jamaica and Nicaragua—was seen in 1952, and no confirmed sightings have been made since.

The Pacific coast has both seals and sea lions. Northern fur seals are mainly found in the cooler waters of the North Pacific, but there is a large, outlying population on San Miguel Island in the Santa Barbara Channel Islands, off the California coast. Fur seal males are huge and competitive, assembling and fighting over harems—a great show for fortunate observers.

The West Coast has two sea lions with overlapping ranges. California sea lions are the kind seen doing tricks in circuses and zoos. It's not clear whether this species is especially easy to train or whether their ready availability to trainers caused them to be selected. They've also been put to use by the U.S. Navy; it is believed that they were involved in the retrieval of a nuclear weapon lost in the sea off the coast of Spain. Whereas the California sea lion is thriving, the ruddy blondish and larger Steller's sea lion has declined, although the cause is not known.

In California, Monterey's wharves often have sea lions around them begging fish handouts. At San Francisco's Pier 39 sea lions haul out and pile up on the docks. Just outside San Francisco Bay sea lions are resident at the dome-shaped rock offshore from Cliff House at Golden State Park. A good place to see harbor seals and sea lions (and coastal elk) is at the Tule Elk Refuge at the northern tip of the Point Reyes Peninsula. And there is a seal rookery at Jenner, California, where the Russian River meets the Pacific.

In Oregon, Three Arch Rocks near Oceanside is a fine sea-lion-watching spot. At Yaquina Head, Oregon, stairs descend from the lighthouse to a hidden beach where you can watch harbor seals on an offshore reef. Sea Lion Cave near Florence, Oregon, supports a large colony of Steller's sea lions. From Cape Arago State Park in Oregon you can, with binoculars, watch Steller's sea lions and harbor seals on Shell Island, a quarter mile to sea. And recently, elephant seals, too—thought to be extinct in the 1880s after rampant overharvesting for their blubber, which, when tried, yielded an oil second in quality only to whale blubber.

A dramatic recovery brought elephant seal numbers from around 20 to 125,000 as of 1994. These huge beasts can reach fifteen feet and more than two tons, and are among the great divers of the sea, sometimes descending about a mile while hunting squid. The elephant-nosed males engage in fierce combat during breeding season, rearing their bodies up and slamming each other while slashing with their large canine teeth. In 1997 they bred successfully on Shell Island, Oregon, extending the giant seal's current range north from California. In California look for elephant seals at Año Nuevo State Beach and the Piedras Blancas beaches in San Simeon where they come ashore to breed, and on the Fallaron, San Miguel, and Los Coronados Islands.

A favorite sea lion haul-out site in British Columbia is the "hulks"—ten old ships that were anchored, ballasted, and chained together at Powell River to make an unusual floating breakwater. Vancouver Island's entire west coast has seals and sea lions in high abundances. Steller's sea lions have a favorite haul-out on Sea Lion Rock near Combers Beach. Killer whales prowl this area for sea lions. California sea lions are common at Wya Point at the end of Florencia Bay.

For truly adventurous pinniped fans, there is a third main category, the walruses. But walruses are boreal species, occurring in the Bering and Chuchki Seas off Alaska, and off Labrador and north to Greenland. Dominance battles among walruses are particularly exciting because they spar with their tusks. These same tusks also come in handy as a fifth limb when crawling out of the water onto an ice floe.

SEA OTTERS
Most playful mammals

Sea otters are the mammalian clowns of the coastal Pacific—they are cute, smallish, and playful mammals with large eyes and a variety of beguiling behaviors, including tool use. The otter feeds on bivalves; it may pull an abalone off the bottom together with a stone, come to the surface and roll over on its back, and then hammer the shellfish against the rock to quickly open it and gouge out the meat. After eating, they may float on their backs and take siestas, and then may bathe and groom to keep their fur in order so that it continues to insulate in the cold sea. To look for danger they rest vertically in the water and shade their eyes with both forefeet. They are often seen with hind flippers extended, as if catching the breeze to sail or drift before it. Sea otters will also dunk a neighbor and steal its food, and play a game akin to leapfrog.

Usually sea otters stay close to shore, but sometimes they are found as far as three miles out. They rest in kelp forests, in groups called rafts. Often they will drape kelp over their bodies like anchor lines to keep from drifting away.

It's possible that two hundred years ago, a million otters ranged along six thousand miles of Pacific coastline from northern Japan to Baja Mexico. But because of their exceptional fur, the thickest of any mammal with up to one million hairs per square inch, hundreds of thousands of these easy marks were killed—wealthy Russians, Spaniards, and

Chinese would wear no other furs. The last southern sea otter herd held on near the Monterey Peninsula, with no more seen after 1831. Extinction was taken as a given; a scientific article published in London in 1938 stated that it is "regrettable that no authentic picture of a sea otter herd will ever be taken. . . ."

But on March 19, 1938, Howard Sharpe looked out to sea at the kelp beds through a telescope from the porch of his home south of Carmel, California, and saw about three hundred small, sleek fur-bearing bodies that clearly weren't the usual seals or sea lions. This was such an extraordinary sight that when he reported it to members of the California Fish and Game Commission, the Hopkins Marine Station, and three newspapers, he was met with skepticism and even amusement. Even a second personal call on the Fish and Game Commission resulted in the same response, but the next day a party of four from that agency showed up at Sharpe's house. It took them a while to believe what they were seeing, but within a short time, news of this remarkable discovery spread around the world. One great mystery remains, though—where did a colony of southern sea otters survive unnoticed for 107 years?

Northern sea otters never declined to crisis levels, and they still roam the North Pacific rim. But now they are threatened by an ecological imbalance that has focused the unwanted attention of a major predator on them. Killer whales normally fed heavily on Steller's sea lions and Pacific harbor seals. But because populations of these prey items have declined, killer whales are hunting more inshore, where they are estimated to have killed between forty and forty-five thousand sea otters since 1990. Researchers believe a single whale can eat almost two thousand otters per year. And the loss of sea otters causes another imbalance to echo through the ecosystem. Sea urchins are the major predators of kelp. When sea otters decline, the urchins thrive, devouring the kelp forests.

Today southern sea otters range from just north of Santa Cruz to near Point Conception, California. Gull congregations sometimes mark sea otters as they hang around the mammals looking for leftovers. The Leffingwell Landing Trail in San Simeon, California, is touted as a good sea-otter-viewing location, as are a number of spots around the Monterey Peninsula. But many consider Point Lobos Reserve, south of Carmel, to be the premier watching station. Certain West Coast cruise ships offer "sea otter and wildlife quests," one even providing a rebate if nary a sea otter, whale, or brown bear is spotted.

SEA TURTLES

Gentle reptilian giants

For anyone who's kept little pet turtles, the sight of a sea turtle is something of a shock—a highly mobile reptile at home in ocean waters and orders of magnitude larger than the one on their bedside table. In fact, the largest of the clan, the leatherback, may reach sixteen hundred pounds.

Five of the eight sea turtles of the world are found in U.S. waters: the leatherback, green, hawksbill, loggerhead, and Kemp's ridley. All but the Kemp's ridley nest on beaches from Virginia to Florida.

Sea turtles were once very abundant in U.S. and Caribbean waters. Many a sailing ship returned to Europe with holds full of green turtles, which provided the only fresh meat for the crew on such voyages. Today these turtles are far scarcer, having been depleted by development that has eradicated nesting habitat, fatalities on the beaches from off-road vehicles, raccoon predation on nests, and from being drowned when caught in commercial fishermen's trawl nets. Indeed, seven of the eight kinds of sea turtles are considered in danger of extinction under the Convention on International Trade in Endangered Species.

Sea turtles must come to the surface to take air, and so they are visible throughout their range to boaters, and sometimes to beachgoers. The presence of jellyfish, one of their favorite foods, in the upper part of the water column also makes sightings frequent. Sea turtles prefer warm waters but range on the East Coast during summer to Newfoundland. They navigate the oceans using the earth's magnetic field; their skulls are packed with millions of ferromagnetic crystals that help create a biological compass. Much as do other animal navigators such as homing pigeons, porpoises, and tuna, it is believed they move about the oceans orienting to magnetic anomalies of the seafloor.

There are two times in their life cycles when sea-turtle-watching is especially compelling. One is the act of egg laying. In general, sea turtle females crawl ashore onto oceanside sand beaches at night sometime in spring or summer. Individuals may repeat the egg-laying process multiple times over a two-week period, depositing, in the case of loggerheads, an average of 120 per visit about eighteen inches deep in the sand. Unfortunately, the quantity and quality of nesting habitat have declined with shore development and recreation; at Cape Hatteras loggerhead and leatherback turtles became disoriented amid deeply rutted trails, and some do not succeed in nesting.

The other exciting event is when baby sea turtles hatch. After incubating for about sixty days, loggerhead turtle hatchlings use a special temporary tooth on their bills to break through the shell of their eggs. At night the vulnerable young burst through the sand above and head toward the bright horizon created by the surf, to remain at sea for the rest of their lives in the case of males and until their first egg-laying bout, for females. But survival rates at this time are very low—less than 1 percent make it to maturity, and much of the mortality occurs soon after hatching. On the beach, large ghost crabs and seabirds dine on the hatchlings. Bluefish, jacks, and sharks may attack when the turtles enter the waves. Divers who've swum behind the young turtles on moonlit nights have seen schools of snappers rise off the bottom to snare the little turtles.

The once numerous green turtle is scarce in U.S. waters today, being seen mainly around the Florida Keys, which also is the most likely U.S. location to see a hawksbill turtle. Greens nest at Fort Lauderdale, Palm Beach, and on the Dry Tortugas—small freshwater-impoverished islands southwest of the Florida Keys. (Ponce de León found these islands in 1513 and named them for their chief inhabitants—sea turtles.) Leatherback turtles are occasionally sighted along the Atlantic coast, but their numbers are down. They belong to a different turtle genus, whose Latin name *Dermochelys* means "skin turtle," which describes the tough leathery hide that serves as their shell. These turtles have lengthy flippers and a long tapered body built for speed (if *turtle* and *speed* aren't oxymoronic), and they prefer deep tropical waters.

The most common sea turtle along the mid-Atlantic is the loggerhead. They nest on certain undeveloped shores between southern Virginia's Back Bay National Wildlife Refuge and Cape Sable in Everglades National Park, and in the Caribbean; several thousand visit the Chesapeake Bay every year, especially in the lower bay, but also near Kent Island and the Choptank River.

The Kemp's ridley is the world's smallest sea turtle, weighing only a hundred pounds at maturity. It nests only on a short stretch of shore at Tamaulipas, Mexico. When they were still abundant in the 1940s, forty thousand females would come ashore as a great mass at once known as *arribadas*. But so many drowned in the nets of commercial shrimpers that by the mid-1980s, nesting females numbered only five hundred. Many half-grown ridleys turn up cold-shocked in northern waters such as Long Island Sound and Boston Harbor, and they are the most common of stray turtles off Nova Scotia. In fact, ridleys and leatherbacks are sometimes found dead in winter along New England shores, presumably from the cold. To rescue cold-shocked turtles along Cape Cod Bay, volunteers comb its beaches in autumn; in 1999 they found 220 Kemp's ridleys.

A good area for spotting sea turtles outside breeding season is near Palm Beach; the Gulf Stream comes in closer to Palm Beach than anywhere along the coast—sometimes its blue transparent waters actually wash over its beaches. The area's reefs host loggerheads as well as both resident and migratory hawksbills, and greens, leatherbacks, and ridleys also are seen.

❧❧❧

SHARK ATTACKS
Galeophobics beware

This is a phenomenon most mariners would rather not witness. Fortunately, shark attacks on humans are not all that frequent in U.S. waters. Stinging insects and snakes kill more people than sharks do. Death from lightning is thirty times more frequent, and there are a thousand drownings for every shark attack. Yet few natural threats evoke the sheer horror of the shark attack—the human, outside his element, relatively helpless, targeted by a swift, streamlined predator that may weigh hundreds of pounds, and whose jaws are arrayed with multitudinous teeth with the sharpness of knives. This fear of sharks even has its own clinical name: galeophobia.

Sharks have long terrorized those who enter the seas. In the third century B.C. Leonidas of Tarentum told of a sponge diver, Tharsys, who lost the lower half of his body to a shark; the poet noted that Tharsys was buried "both on land and sea." Around A.D. 77 Pliny the Elder wrote about the "vast numbers of sharks" infesting the sea around sponge beds "to the great peril of those who dive for them." Sharks terrified seamen in the Mediterranean during the eighteenth century; believing that a sighted shark would not attack except in hunger, the sailors would toss it a loaf of bread to placate it.

The beachside shark scare portrayed in the movie *Jaws* was inspired by a real one that occurred in New Jersey in 1916. Within twelve days two swimmers were killed in the ocean, probably by a great white shark, and two attacks with one fatality took place in a small creek, presumably by a bull shark. The unprecedented concentration of attacks led to a fright that spread from Rhode Island to Florida. Earlier, Thoreau had put succinctly the ubiquity of sharks in human-inhabited regions: "Serpents, bears, hyenas, tigers, rapidly vanish as civilization advances, but the most populous and civilized city cannot scare a shark from its wharves."

Worldwide, most shark attacks have been made by the same three species: great white, tiger, and bull sharks. The first two are denizens of ocean waters and shores; bull sharks are typically found in river mouths and estuaries. In the United States mako, blue, and blacktip sharks also are among those that have attacked people, and all sharks should be considered dangerous and treated with respect.

Not all shark attacks continue beyond the initial assault. Many can be classified as "hit-and-run" attacks in which the curious shark inflicts a single bite or slash wound and then departs; these attacks can nevertheless be fatal, however, depending on whether vital organs are hit or blood loss is quickly stemmed.

Research has shown that shark attacks near shore are most frequent in late morning and late afternoon. Swimmers and divers at the surface are more prone to shark attacks than divers in the mid-depths or at the bottom. Surfers are struck far more frequently than either swimmers or divers. Color may play a role; sharks seem to be attracted to bright hues—the standard color of life jackets has become known as "yum-yum yellow" among shark researchers.

Shark attacks are more common in warmer waters where sharks are more numerous and there are more shark species; most sharks live in waters of sixty-eight degrees Fahrenheit or higher (but great whites have been found as far north as Newfoundland). Countervailing forces have dictated the frequency of shark attacks: More people are recreating in the water these days with the growing popularity of surfing, kayaking, and Jet Skiing. For the most part, however, sharks have declined along our shores because of overfishing. They once were much more common in inshore waters; in the mid- to late 1800s they even were numerous along Manhattan's wharves, where they fed on dumped refuse.

Data from 1959 to 1990 show 336 known shark attacks in U.S. waters, with more than half occurring in Florida. The 180 attacks in Florida, however, resulted in four fatalities, whereas 59 attacks in California resulted in six deaths—the higher proportion largely due to the predominance of great white sharks in the West Coast attacks. In fact, the large majority of shark attacks in U.S. waters occurred in

Florida, California, and Hawaii, and instances were scarce from Virginia northward.

There are three areas in the United States that swimmers and surfers should be especially aware of. Although southern Florida's Palm Beach County once held the distinction, the epicenter of Florida's shark attacks today is Volusia County, along the state's central east coast. In 1998 fourteen of twenty-two Floridian assaults occurred in such famous Volusia County beaches as Daytona, Ormond, and New Smyrna. But Volusia County's preeminence is partly due to its recent growth—there are more people in the water. Ironically, and somewhat defensively, too, New Smyrna Beach was calling itself "The World's Safest Beach" because sandbars running parallel with the shore were thought to keep sharks away. But in 2000, there were a number of attacks there, including two each on two separate days— though none was fatal. In 2001 a Florida-based episode received considerable attention when a bull shark attacked an eight-year-old boy near Pensacola. But the boy's uncle wrestled the shark to shore and retrieved the boy's arm from the fish's jaws, enabling surgeons to reattach it.

Off California there is a region so associated with shark attacks that it is known as "the Red Triangle"—from Bodega Bay southward to the Farallon Islands, to the mainland near Santa Cruz. Records show that from 1952 to 1999, there were seventy-nine shark attacks in West Coast waters; forty-one of them were within the Red Triangle. Researchers believe that many of these attacks are due to sharks confusing humans with various kinds of seals and sea lions, their prevalent prey in these waters.

Dead floating whales are also shark magnets, because they easily zero in on the scent of the massive hunk of flesh. Recently, in Australia, some individuals exercised the epitome of poor judgment in hopping from a boat onto a large whale and then petting the dozen great white sharks that were chomping literally inches from their feet. Although no one died in this instance, Australian authorities are now considering banning people from within about a hundred-yard radius of dead whales "to protect people too stupid to protect themselves."

Sharks have long held an important role in Hawaiian lore; Native Hawaiians even had a special word for sharks that eat people: *niuhi*. In recent decades the majority of shark attacks in Hawaii have taken place around the islands of Oahu and Maui. Just as great whites rule Californian waters, in Hawaii tiger sharks are the chief instigators of galeophobia.

And there is some good news concerning shark attacks: A study of more than a thousand cases in the International Shark Attack File showed that the chances of surviving an attack are better than even, at 65 percent.

∽∾∽

SHARK'S TEETH
Cutting-edge beachcombing

Fossilized shark's teeth are an especially compelling beach find—and they are not as rare as you might expect. This is because the teeth that are found are not only the re-sult of shark deaths in antiquity. Sharks, while alive, shed and replace their teeth on a regular basis—the young of one shark species replace their upper teeth every seven days, and their lower teeth every eight days. Individuals may produce as many as twenty thousand teeth in their lifetime. Once on the seafloor, the teeth mineralize, picking up the colors of the sands and silts they become buried in.

Shark River, New Jersey, is so called because of the fossil shark teeth commonly found upstream in its freshwater source. Shark's teeth can often be found nearby at the ocean at Belmar, where typically one-half- to three-quarter-inch teeth appear on the surface of the sand.

Maryland's Calvert Cliffs on the western shore of the Chesapeake Bay offer superb fossil hunting and are noted for shark's teeth. The fossil deposits of the cliffs are from the seafloor of millions of years ago (sharks existed before trees), but they now stand about a hundred feet above the waterline. Wave action continually undermines the cliffs, liberating fossils that are cleaned by the sea and tossed back on shore by the surf.

Species of shark that left teeth at Calvert Cliffs include tiger, sand, hammerhead, mako, silky, and snaggle-tooth sharks, with the occasional outsized tooth from the giant white shark, which reached forty feet in Miocene times—or about double the size of great white sharks today. The exceptional abundance of teeth at Calvert Cliffs cannot be explained only by their routine shedding. The predominance of bones of young whales may mean that this site was a calving ground, and that many of these bones are marked with bites suggests that sharks were drawn to the area.

Venice, on Florida's Gulf of Mexico coast, is known in typical chamber of commerce lingo as the "Shark Tooth Mecca of the World." The teeth found near Venice are millions of years old and range in length from one-eighth of an inch to three inches, but any over an inch are rare. A recommended search technique is to scan the water being washed by the waves for the flat teeth sliding back with the outwash.

Although shark teeth are a common fossil, don't expect to find shark bones—the rest of the shark skeleton is cartilage, not bone, and this softer material doesn't preserve well.

~~~

SHELL COLLECTING

Rare beauty at your feet

"A good shell can distill time and place, like a good poem, and seems worth wet feet," wrote Jennifer Ackerman in *Notes from the Shore*. Millions of beachcombers would agree.

Most of the shells found on beaches are from mollusks, of which there are eighty to one hundred thousand species in the world. These divide chiefly into bivalves (paired shells), such as clams and abalone, and gastropods, including snails, whelks, and conchs. But bivalves don't always come as paired halves. Most often this is simply due to the hinge between them separating as they tumble over the sea bottom. But one of my favorite bivalves is the jingle shell *Anomia simplex*, which is never found on shore in its paired shell form because its bottom member is so strongly cemented to rocks that it never breaks free; only the upper shells are found. These mother-of-pearl shells "jingle," making a tinkling sound as they roll in the wash; they're also known as "mermaid's toes."

Shell hunting differs in each of the three main zones of tidal beaches. In the supratidal zone, the area of dry sand high on the beach, the best technique is simply to stroll, making sure to poke around in any piles of stranded debris such as seaweed drifts. The intertidal zone usually offers the best rewards, with fresh shells often left behind by high tides, so it can be especially fruitful to search on a falling tide. The subtidal zone isn't often exposed, but may be when a strong offshore wind pushes water seaward. It's also possible to wade and find shells in the subtidal zone if the water is clear. A good rule to follow is that shelling and all forms of beachcombing are best soon after storms, which stir the sea and toss up collectibles of all kinds.

The mostly bedrock New England coast offers fewer beaches than to the south. In fact, Maine only has sixty-five miles of sand and gravel beach—about 2 percent of its rugged shoreline. In *The Art of Shelling*, the Robinsons recommend the Petit Manan Wildlife Refuge at Steuben in Downeast Maine. It offers mainly sea urchins, mussels, limpets, and periwinkles; some of the beaches in its coves are colored in pastel pinks and blues because they are composed almost completely of periwinkle or mussel shells. At this beach the authors even found lobster pots, buoys, and a note in a bottle from someone in Texas.

Although a really high diversity of shells is more typical of southern waters, Cape Cod offers many of the temperate standards, plus rarer ones, and some with evocative names such as blood ark, lunar dove shell, well-ribbed dove shell, solitary paper bubble, Gould's pandora, and the tiny amethyst gem clam, once collected by colonists and shipped to Europe to be embroidered on clothing.

Ocracoke Island, part of North Carolina's Outer Banks, offers superior shelling. Among its specialties are lettered olives—glossy, cylindrical shells with zigzag markings—and Scotch bonnets, whelklike shells with rows of dark, squarish spots. Neither comes easily, though; it may take days to find a few unbroken specimens. But not all of the shells evident on a beach are necessarily recent. Most shells on North Carolina beaches have been radiocarbon dated to nine thousand years ago and originally came from the sounds and lagoons in back of the beaches, and so should be considered fossils.

Florida offers outstanding shelling opportunities. Because of the greater surf action, the shells of its east coast are more often damaged than those found on its Gulf of Mexico shores. Florida's northeast coast does not have high shell diversity, but it is an excellent area for angel wings—lovely four- to eight-inch shells that look just like their name suggests. Farther south, near Dania, the beaches are strong on deep-water shells, such as lion's paw and kitten's paw, and for a variety of interestingly marked scallops, including calicos and zigzags.

The Florida Keys are an attractive shelling locale, partly because it is where two shell faunas meet—the Carolinian Province, which extends northward, and the tropical Caribbean Province. Although beaches are scarce on the mostly rocky or mangrove-lined keys, some have large numbers of truly miniature shells, ranging between one-eighth and one-sixteenth inch.

Sanibel Island on Florida's west coast offers what many consider to be the best shell collecting in the United States, and ranks among the top ten locations in the world. Because it juts out into the Gulf of Mexico rather than stretching in parallel with the mainland like most barrier islands, Sanibel forms a barricade to the predominant currents, piling shells there. And the possibilities are numerically spectacular. Almost three hundred kinds of mollusks live in the nearby shallows. Five hundred more species occur in the eighty- to two-thousand-foot depths. And almost one thousand more forms are found deeper offshore, on the eighty-mile-wide continental shelf. The prize among all of these is the junonia—a beautiful spiral-shelled snail with winding rows of square-shaped brown spots on a creamy background. Its rarity stems in part from its source—junonia is a deep-water mollusk. Although less well-known, Dog Island in the northern Gulf of Mexico is also an excellent shell-collecting spot, as is Marco Island, which leans strongly toward bivalves, with gastropods scarce.

The West Coast has a high diversity of shells, with about five thousand species found between Alaska and Panama. *Pitar* is an unusual kind, having fine calcareous projections along one edge. Monterey's Fanshell Beach is named for the many fanshells that wash up after winter storms, although they are usually picked clean by summer.

∽∾∾

SHOREBIRD MIGRATIONS
Hemisphere hoppers

Shorebirds are small, brownish birds that make a living on ocean shores, sandbars, and mudflats. Among them are plovers, turnstones, sandpipers, curlews, and phalaropes. Physically they are not imposing or even especially interesting; for the most part, they resemble each other—what bird-watchers call "LBJs" or little brown jobs. (Bird-watchers have their own lingo, including identifying a bird by its jizz, borrowed from the fighter pilot's acronym *GIS*, for "general impression and shape.") No, what makes shorebirds special are their habits, appearance in numbers, and mighty migrations.

These habits are worth watching. Harry Thurston, in *The Nature of Shorebirds*, described the aerial maneuvers of one shorebird species: "Sandpipers flow and turn together with such uncanny precision as to make one think they are a single organism." Dowitchers rapidly move their long straight bills up and down in a sewing-machine motion as they probe mudflats. And sanderlings are entertaining as they feed along the edge of waves, retreating before them, and then speed-walking to pick food particles as they recede.

Many shorebirds make the annual trip to South America to winter, then back to the East Coast, particularly Canada, to summer. Such dramatic "habitat switching," as also occurs for neotropical songbirds and for salmon that are born high in rivers but live at sea, is seen throughout the vertebrate world, and it sometimes appears incongruous with the organism's size or simply not worth it from the human point of view. But it is a truism among ecologists that the cost-to-benefit ratios must be favorable or the habitat-switching behaviors wouldn't evolve. Both the bioenergetic demands on a tiny bird to fly many hundreds or thousands of miles and its level of exposure to predation are immense. But the cost of remaining in the wrong hemisphere during winter and attempting to continuously feed a small, rapidly respiring body from a scant food supply is greater. Yes, the travel circuit is demanding, but at least the food is assured to be there on each end of the trip.

A major fast-food strip on the migratory highway is Delaware Bay in spring, where after winging it from the distal reaches of South America, shorebirds stop and feast on horseshoe crab eggs, famished after having flown nonstop from South America for as many as three days. Many of these birds still have more than a thousand miles to fly to the Arctic tundra and so they fatten up, each bird over two or three weeks increasing its weight by 40 percent or more. Estimates are that sanderlings each eat nine thousand eggs per day and together, a total of twenty-seven tons per season—and that doesn't include what's taken by their competitors, the red knots and ruddy turnstones. The popularity of this stop is attested to by the numbers of birds making it; biologists have observed as many as 350,000 shorebirds in a two-hour survey of Delaware Bay. It is believed that at least 80 percent of the shorebirds in eastern North America pause there.

Another excellent place to see shorebirds where they gather in great numbers is the Bay of Fundy. Walk out on the bay's extensive mudflats at low tide and you'll see why millions of these birds return: The ooze teems with tiny shrimplike animals—twenty to sixty thousand per square meter. The shorebirds arrive at the Bay of Fundy in July and fatten up—individual birds may eat twenty thousand shrimp each day. But they burn these energy reserves when they stream back twenty-four hundred miles to South America, making the trip in seventy-two hours, nonstop. Many thousands also summer in the Nauset Marsh on Cape Cod and other lesser estuaries. The West Coast has its own suite of migratory shorebirds, including curlews, dowitchers, willets, sandpipers, and killdeers.

An elite subset of shorebirds make the world's longest migrations. Nineteen species breed north of the Arctic Circle; every one of them visits South America in winter, six of them penetrating to Patagonia, an extraordinary migration route more than eight thousand miles in length.

SINGING SANDS
A "note" worthy phenomenon

It has long been realized that under certain conditions in particular locations you can hear the "song of the sands"; the singing sands of the Island of Eigg in the Hebrides are famous. These sounds are most often associated with dunes and sandbanks. Sometimes sands piled high by winds yield a musical tone while sliding back down the incline.

Sands also make tonal sounds when walked over, struck by foot, or stroked by hand. They've been described as sounding vaguely like human voices singing, or akin to a faint violin. This phenomenon was studied by two college professors in 1884 at the so-called singing beach at Manchester, Massachusetts. The sounds that could be obtained by friction on this beach were decidedly musical, and the investigators were able to chart the exact notes on a musical staff. They found that the shrillness or lowness of the note depended on the quantity of sand disturbed. By rubbing a large handful of the sand vigorously, several notes on a rising scale could be heard, the notes rising as the amount of sand between the hands diminished. The notes were not discerned separately, but with the impression formed by sliding a finger up a violin string at the same time the bow is drawn. The two professors then tested the sands at Far Rockaway Beach in New York but did not register low notes there.

The exact mechanism of how sands sing is not known. But it has been discovered that singing sands are polished, free from fragments, and nearly all within a narrow range of size.

On the West Coast, sands sometimes sing at the Oregon Dunes National Recreation Area.

∽∾∽

SOFTSHELL OR "STEAMER" CLAMS
Aka "piss," long neck, gaper, and nannynose clams

Rachel Carson said that when she walked over the sands, she felt as if she "were treading on the thin rooftops of an underground city." No sea creature makes clear the metropolis that lies below quite like *Mya arenaria*, a clam that announces its presence from deep beneath the muddy sand it dwells in. Walk along a softshell-clam-inhabited beach and you'll see jets of water shooting upward a foot or two, like little geysers, sometimes as a quick squirt, other times as a long fountain. These mark the burrows of individual clams, resting inches to more than a foot below.

Softshell clams occur mainly between the high- and low-tide marks. They feed by elevating their long, tough "necks," which contain two siphons, allowing them to pass food-bearing water through their bodies. Softshell clams are delicious, although aficionados are divided into two camps: those who eat the whole clam and those who discard the rubbery necks. These clams range naturally from Labrador to North Carolina. One of their names, *nannynose*, may be a corruption of *manninose*—the Native American name for them in the Chesapeake Bay area. Softshell clams were introduced to California around 1865 or 1870, and now extend in West Coast waters from central California to British Columbia.

Although softshell clams appear to shoot water periodically on their own, the vibrations from footsteps, probably interpreted to mean a possible predator above, causes them to contract their long neck for safety, forcing water out in the process. There are few young children who are not delighted to stamp around on top of a bed of piss clams to make them spout.

SPINY LOBSTER MARCHES
Crustaceans in single file

Every autumn the great saltwater crayfish march occurs in tropical American waters. For observers, this most reliably occurs off Bimini, just after the first autumn cold fronts cool the shallows. First the spiny lobsters assemble, massing together and milling about. Hundreds to some-

times thousands of spiny lobsters then parade along open sandy bottoms in great chains, the links made of two to sixty lobsters, each individual overlapping its antennae with the tail of the animal in front. When they stop on their way, they form defensive circles with their sharp antennae facing outward. These chains snake their way off to warmer waters at the edge of the continental shelf. Migrations may be as far as a hundred miles, at a rate of about a mile per day.

STINGRAYS

Graceful swordsmen

Stingrays are flattened relatives of sharks whose broad winglike fins allow them to gracefully glide through the water. The *sting* in *stingray* derives from the large, hard, movable spine composed of dentine that is attached midway down their tails. It can reach a daggerlike six inches in some species. If a stingray is stepped upon, it swings its tail over its back, lacerating the flesh with its saw-edged spine and introducing venom through two long grooves. This can result in agonizing pain and swelling, vomiting, sweating, an elevated heart rate, and sometimes—but rarely—death. The wound also is extremely slow to heal, and they've been long known to cause "gangrene of the wounded flesh." Fortunately, there are only about fifteen hundred stingray attacks in the United States each year. Despite the very real dangers from stingrays, their powers were exaggerated by Pliny the Elder, who claimed that a stingray could kill a tree by driving its sting into one of the roots.

Captain John Smith learned about stingrays the hard way, writing upon a visit in 1608 to the Chesapeake Bay:

> It came to pass that I had pierced a very-curiously shaped fish, and knowing nothing about it, was taking it off the point of my sword as I had done others. It was much of the fashion of a thornback, with a long tail like a riding whip, in the midst whereof is a most poisonous sting of two or three inches long, bearded like a saw on either side. This the fish stuck into my wrist, to the depth of near an inch and a half; no blood issued forth, nor could any wound be seen, except a little blue spot, but the torment was instantly extreme, by reason of its poison, and in four hours' time my hand, arm, and shoulder had swollen to such a size, and my agony was so great, that I concluded that my death was indeed nigh, and this, my opinion, was shared by the whole company.

Smith went on to have a grave dug for him, but the pain passed and he became hungry, eating his tormentor. (Captain Smith certainly was not lucky with his health while in the Chesapeake Bay. The next year a gunpowder bag suspended from his belt incinerated and burned a hole in his leg, again bringing expectation of death, but he again survived.)

A stingray known as the cownose is very abundant in the Chesapeake, where it travels in groups of as many as two hundred. These large fish with up to forty-five-inch wingspans sometimes beat the water, making great crashing noises. Although they seem to be cavorting, they actually are using rapid wing movements to churn bottom sediment and expose buried clams and other shellfish. Cownose rays are not as dangerous as other stingrays because they are usually swimming, not lying on the sand, and thus are less likely to be stepped on. When wading anywhere in stingray country, however, it's wise to wear sneakers or water shoes and to shuffle your feet to drive stingrays out of the sediment before you come down on them.

On the Pacific coast the beach at California's Glorietta Bay near San Diego can be home to large numbers of stingrays, especially early in the season before prolonged human activity has driven them out. One guidebook on the area tried unsuccessfully to be reassuring, stating that "the sting only seems fatal."

SWORDFISH ATTACKS ON VESSELS

A strange threat to mariners

With its cosmopolitan distribution, aggressive demeanor, and historically high abundance, the swordfish is legendary among mariners. The often repeated tales of terrific combats between whales and swordfish, the latter sometimes aided by the long-tailed thresher shark, are almost certainly apocryphal. But there is evidence that sword-

fish do occasionally ram whales, and there is no doubt that they have attacked ships. And these billfish are formidable, often weighing more than a hundred pounds and known to reach sixteen feet and eleven hundred pounds.

In 1674 a European, John Josselyn, when returning from New England witnessed a large swordfish pierce his ship and then break off its sword while wriggling to break loose. Much earlier Pliny, the Roman naturalist, wrote that the swordfish ". . . hath a beake or bill sharp pointed, where-with he will drive through the sides and plankes of a ship, and gouge them so, that they shall sinke withall."

When the whale ship *Fortune* returned to Plymouth, Massachusetts, in 1828, the stump of a swordfish blade was noticed projecting from the hull. When traced, it was found to have been driven through the external copper sheathing, an inch-thick wooden undersheathing, a three-inch-thick plank of hardwood, a solid white oak timber one foot thick, and a two-and-a-half-inch hard oak ceiling, lastly penetrating the head of an oil cask, where it stuck, not allowing a drop of oil to escape.

In 1919 a swordfish schooner had to return to its Boston port after a billfish pierced its planking, several inches of the spear protruding through the ship's forecastle. After the swordfish was killed at sea, it was necessary to saw away the sword, leaving it embedded in the craft. One theory for these attacks is that the fish experience "fits of temporary insanity." But it is also possible that they ram ships accidentally as they pursue prey that darts near the vessels for shelter.

More commonly, swordfish attack a fishing vessel after the fish has been harpooned. Over the years several fishermen have been wounded in the leg after billfish pierced the bottoms of dory skiffs.

Sometimes hooked swordfish and other billfish leap during battle and land on their hunter's vessels, where they cause extensive damage with their bills or simply by thrashing about. Recently a fisherman near Acapulco, Mexico, was fighting a ten-foot marlin when the fish jumped and speared him in the abdomen, with its bill exiting the man's back. The fisherman, unable to get up, drifted for two days until another vessel rescued him.

TIDES

The heavens pull and the oceans follow

Although the Roman naturalist Pliny was born in A.D. 23 he wrote one of the best and most succinct explanations of the tides to date. In *Historia Naturalis* he stated:

> *Much has been said about the nature of waters; but the most wonderful circumstance is the alternate flowing and ebbing of the tides, which exist, indeed, under various forms, but is*

caused by the sun and the moon. The tide flows twice and ebbs twice between each two risings of the moon, always in the space of twenty-four hours. First, the moon rising with the stars swells out the tide, and after some time, having gained the summit of the heavens, she declines from the meridian and sets, and the tide subsides. Again, after she has set, and moves the heavens under the earth, as she approaches the meridian on the opposite side, the tide flows in; after which it recedes until she again rises to us. But the tide of the next day is never at the same time with that of the preceding.

Although the ancients had a generally good grasp on the tides, legend has it that Aristotle, in his dotage, despaired that he couldn't explain why a particular Greek channel's tide changed every three hours (a phenomenon that remains unexplained).

As incongruous as it may seem for such an earthly phenomenon, tides are due solely to the pull of two celestial objects: the sun and the moon. That great unseen force, gravity, tugs at the world's waters, causing them to bulge upward when the attraction is strongest and to recede when the gravitational attraction lessens. But how this puckering of the sea expresses itself is complicated by the rotation of the earth and the fact that water doesn't simply lie evenly over the globe but is distributed in ocean basins, bays, sounds, creeks, and straits that cause many interesting anomalies.

The "prince of tides" is the Bay of Fundy in Maritime Canada. The tidal range at the mouth of the Bay of Fundy is large but not unusual—about nine and a half feet maximum. On every high tide, however, some twenty-four cubic miles of water flow into the bay—a volume equal to the daily discharge of the world's rivers combined. This surge pushes up a bay that narrows down to two basins at its head; water piles up as it has less room. At the end of one terminus, the Chignecto Basin, the tide is forty-six feet; at the end of its other terminus, the Minas Basin, tides can exceed fifty feet.

One tide at the head of the Bay of Fundy reached fifty-six feet on October 5, 1869—the famous Saxby Tides, so called because such an extremely high tide had been predicted eleven months before by a Lieutenant Saxby of the British Royal Navy, and apparently without adequate scientific rationale. The Bay of Fundy's tides can be augmented by southwest winds, which may add as much as another six feet of water.

For anyone who is accustomed to the three- to eight-foot tides that are found around much of North America, the routine tidal changes of the Bay of Fundy are an astonishing sight. I once visited a marsh on the bay's northeastern shore. When the tide began to go out, it ebbed at such a speed that each succeeding wavelet struck the shore at a lower mark. At full ebb, the northern arms of the bay are vast reddish flats with a thin band of water draining through its lowest point. But as the tide reverses, sheets of water surge inland, pools expand, and any waters still draining are subsumed by the massive incoming flow.

Tidal swings are dependent on underwater topography, though, and sometimes this hinders them. Not far from the Bay of Fundy is Nova Scotia's salty Lake Bras d'Or. Although it is immense and deep and connected to the sea by two channels that allow fish and ships to pass, minimal water transfer restrains tides to a few inches.

To the south, tides average about nine feet at Cape Cod, but only a foot and a half offshore at Nantucket Island, six feet in New York Harbor, about three or four feet from Cape Cod to Cape Hatteras, and only a little over two feet in the

Gulf of Mexico. Alaskan tides are routinely twenty feet and more. Some West Coast locations have mixed tides—two sets of tides each day of different amplitudes. In places where these occur, sometimes a lower high water is followed by a higher low water, resulting in a "vanishing tide" where the level remains fairly constant for several hours.

Tides are easily predicted, and information on highs and lows is readily obtainable. If a local newspaper doesn't present them, consult the venerable *Eldridge Tide and Pilot Book*. The Eldridge family is good at figuring out the tides—four generations have done it in the little yellow-jacketed book since 1875.

TIDAL BORES

Sometimes a bore is exciting

In rivers near sea level tides may advance upriver; tidal effects are felt as much as five hundred miles up the Amazon. In some rivers that grow shallow and narrow in the upriver direction but have large tidal ranges, the advancing tidal wave creates a breaking wall of water—called a bore—that rushes upstream with a front that is sometimes almost vertical. Continually, the water in back overtakes the slower water at the foot of the wave.

Worldwide, some famous rivers have tidal bores: the Amazon (called *Pororoca* or "crashing water"; it can be a fifteen-foot wall), the Indus in India, the Seine and Gironde in France, and the Severn and Trent in England. The bore of the Seine is known as the *mascaret* and once reached the frightening height of twenty-four feet before dredging of the river tamed it somewhat. In some places the bore is used to advantage: Chinese fishermen in the Tsientang Chiang would beach their boats on a sheltered shelf and then use the "after rush" of the bore to travel.

In North America, at the Turnagain and Knik Arms at the head of Cook Inlet, near Anchorage, Alaska, bores reach six feet under low-water conditions. A tidal bore on Nova Scotia's Shubenacadie River is easily observed from a commercial "bore-watching" operation. In Moncton, New Brunswick, on the Petticodiac River, the daily time of arrival of the bore is posted on a city street. Its height is about three feet—sometimes as much as five or six feet— and it approaches with a rushing, roaring sound. In *The Atlantic Shore*, Hay and Farb wrote that ". . . gulls shift to the sides of the river to escape it, and anyone viewing it for the first time might feel that it had an almost uncanny, inexorable power."

TIDAL SYZYGY

When celestial bodies align

Technically, *syzygy* is the term for those two intervals each month when the gravitational fields of the moon and the sun are lined up to work in conjunction on the earth's waters, producing the more pronounced swings in height called "spring" tides seen at the new- and full-moon stages. But *syzygy* is also used to describe what happens when the moon and sun team up to produce highly extreme tides seen only once to several times a decade.

As we may have forgotten since physics class, the gravitational attraction between two bodies varies as the product of their masses and inversely with the square of the distance between their centers. Although the sun is twenty-seven million times larger than the moon, it also is ninety-three million miles away—so many more times less than the quarter-million-mile distance from earth of the moon that despite its supreme size advantage, the sun's influence on the tides is only 46 percent that of the moon's.

The moon's average distance from earth is about 239,000 miles, but with an elliptical orbit it varies between apogee (most distant point) and perigee (nearest point). When the moon is at perigee and the sun and moon are at syzygy, perigean spring tides occur, which may be 40 percent greater than average. In December 1999 the moon at perigee was only about 220,000 miles away, while the earth was nearest its closest possible approach to the sun, producing remarkably high and low tides, now called proxigean spring tides. One such tide that washed the Northeast in late November 1885 produced these headlines (with an old-time flavor not seen today) in the *Boston Herald:* "A MIGHTY TIDE," "Old Neptune Baptizes the Shore," "An Unprecedented Rise of Water," "Great Damage to Property in New York," and "Picturesque Commingling of Wind and Wave."

I once went to my favorite striped bass fishing spot in Long Island Sound at low tide, not knowing that what must have been a proxigean spring tide was occurring. When I arrived at the shallow bay it was as if someone had pulled the plug out of a great bathtub—I was amazed to walk high out of the water over mussel beds and rock reefs whose existence weren't even hinted at on typical spring tides.

TIDE POOLS

Little seas unto themselves

Tide pools are snippets of oceans reduced to ponds or puddles. Whether formed from crevices in the glacial bedrock of Maine or Nova Scotia, or from depressions on long sandy beaches of the Carolinas, or the hard-lava pools of Oregon and California, they are easily accessed and absorbing microcosms of the ecology of the surrounding seas. But they also are unique ecosystems of their own.

Falling tides trap animals in tide pools. For the most part, the creatures temporarily caged are small, less mobile forms, but there are accounts of hefty seagoing fish such as false albacore turning up in tide pools.

Along the rocky coast, there is a hierarchy of tide pools. Those closest to the low-tide line have the shortest exposure times and may harbor the richest diversity of life. Then there are tide pools that are above the high-tide line—these receive their water from waves and splash and are of the least interest inasmuch as they tend to be biologically impoverished, at least in comparison with lower pools. These highest pools are harsh environments: They are not flushed regularly, grow hot in the summer sun, often hold little oxygen, and have broad ranges of salinities as they evaporate in dry periods and become fresh during heavy rains.

For the most part, tide pools will not dazzle the viewer with action. A commitment should be made to relax, be still, and observe. Only then will fish dart around, with careful scanning revealing slow-moving starfish, crabs, and snails, and perhaps rarer creatures going about their business. But the effects of these little forms of life are greater than you might think. Rachel Carson wrote about a California tide pool observed by a biologist who found that the alga-scraping periwinkles lowered the rock floor of the basin by three-eighths of an inch over sixteen years.

John Steinbeck, in *Cannery Row*, provided a précis of California tide pool life:

> *Doc was collecting marine animals in the Great Tide Pool on the tip of the Peninsula. It is a fabulous place: when the tide is in, a wave-churned basin, creamy with foam, whipped by the combers that roll in from the whistling buoy on the reef. But when the tide goes out the little water*

world becomes quiet and lovely. The sea is very clear and the bottom becomes fantastic with hurrying, fighting, feeding, breeding animals. Crabs rush from frond to frond of the waving algae. Starfish squat over mussels and limpets, attach their million little suckers and then slowly lift with incredible power until the prey is broken from the rock. And then the starfish stomach comes out and envelops its food. Orange and speckled and fluted nudibranchs slide gracefully over the rocks, their skirts waving like the dresses of Spanish dancers. And black eels poke their heads out of crevices and wait for prey. The snapping shrimps with their trigger claws pop loudly. The lovely, colored world is glassed over. Hermit crabs like frantic children scamper on the bottom sand. And now one, finding an empty snail shell he likes better than his own, creeps out, exposing his soft body to the enemy for a moment, and then pops into the new shell. A wave breaks over the barrier, and churns the glassy water for a moment and mixes bubbles into the pool, and then it clears and is tranquil and lovely and murderous again.

In New England, Schoodic Point at Acadia National Park has fine tide pools, as does Two Lights Park on Cape Elizabeth, near Portland, Maine, where the receding tide exposes hundreds of pools. Coldwater tide pools from Maine northward may reveal the lumpfish, a slow moving, purse-shaped fish whose roe provides a quality caviar. Odiorne Point State Park in New Hampshire and the Cape Ann area of Massachusetts also provide good tide pooling.

From Long Island southward, tide pools are radically different due to the absence of bedrock. Tide pools will form on sand flats, but they tend to be ephemeral and barren by comparison.

On the Pacific coast you may see giant red sea urchins; splendid iridescent seaweed—a species whose leaflike fronds in flowing waters are said to pulsate and shimmer like the northern lights; or sea palms that look just like miniature palm trees. In California, La Jolla's Bird Rock is said to have the clearest coastal waters in the state, with rich tide pools. The rocky shore at Hazard Canyon near Morro Bay has tide pools large enough for rubber rafts. Large expanses of a long, mostly flat shelf become exposed on extreme low tides. At Cabrillo Beach in Los Angeles, Cabrillo Marine Aquarium naturalists conduct tide pool tours; Los Angeles County's Point Dume offers excellent tide pooling among extended shelflike rocks. Farther north, Ocean City Park, Natural Bridges Beach State Park, Monterey's Pacific Grove Marine Gardens Park, and Stinson Beach all have good, accessible pools.

In Oregon the beaches of Tillamook County are great for tide pooling. Some truly unusual tide pools exist at Yaquina Head, Oregon—they are man-made. The area had been purchased in the 1950s by a gravel company under the almost incomprehensible and certainly archaic 1877 Mining Law, which states that miners can claim and buy almost any federal land with mineral value. The company claimed that gravel was a mineral, bought the headland for just a few dollars an acre, and began to scar the land. But locals objected—in particular Senator Mark Hatfield, who owned a house nearby—and Congress brought it back under federal jurisdiction, but at a price of millions of dollars. The Bureau of Land Management was unsure what to do with this boondoggle but hit upon an inspired scheme: They removed the dikes holding back the sea, paved the trails, and created wheelchair-accessible tide pools.

In Washington there is good tide pooling at Teahwhit Head on the Olympic Peninsula. Someone once claimed

that this is one of the best places in the world to observe intertidal invertebrates because the fog is sometimes so thick
that the animals don't notice the tide has gone out and left
them exposed.

British Columbia has an excellent tide pooling shoreline
at Botanical Beach Provincial Park at Port Renfrew. In these
sculpted sandstone pools have been found more than 230
kinds of plants and one hundred invertebrates.

TOADFISH SONGS AND OTHER FISH SOUNDS

Queer noises from unlikely sources

A peculiar, highly sedentary creature with fleshy flaps
surrounding a broad mouth, the toadfish is among the ugli-
est fish in the sea. Most of the time, toadfish lie camou-
flaged on the bottom. Males build nests under rocks and in
sunken tires; in New York I've found them in burrows above
the low-tide line simply by flipping over large rocks.

One unusual characteristic of toadfish is their vocal-
ization. For weeks, houseboaters in Sausalito, California,
were kept awake at night by mysterious underwater
sounds—the mating call of male toadfish. Likened to a
boat whistle, it is a true song, a particular pattern of notes
made by specialized muscles in the swim bladder. To attract a mate, the song must have just the right frequency
and volume and be sung about seven times per minute.
The singing is highly competitive; when a female arrives,
the males try to outdo each other, and the sea becomes a
chorus of beeps, hoots, and grunts. Although North American toadfish are remarkably noisy despite their usual
foot-long size, a South American species reaches three feet
and is known to roar.

It turns out the sea is a surprisingly noisy place, with a symphony of creatures that communicate by making sounds. A large family of fish called drums received that name because of the characteristic loud drumming or croaking sounds they make when caught. The drum's sound is produced by the rapid contracting of a special muscle that runs along the fish's air bladder, which serves as a resonator. Along the Atlantic coast, a smallish drum called the croaker is the loudest of the group; during World War II the rumbles of croaker schools in the Chesapeake Bay picked up by hydrophones caused the coastal defense network to believe an invasion was occurring.

But many other fish produce sounds, often in physiologically creative ways. Sea robins are remarkably vocal, constantly clucking and squawking. Another family also has a noise-based name—the grunts. Grunts grunt by rubbing specialized teeth together. Triggerfish audibilize by moving two bones in the shoulder area together, with the vibrations resonated by the swim bladder. An ocean sunfish hauled ashore made "hideous groans" by grating the teeth in its throat.

Fish sounds are believed to be made to attract mates or to defend territories. But maybe their purpose is to appeal to the hearts of fishermen—as an angler, I find it hard to keep a fish that is speaking to me.

TRAVELING DUNES
Slow but inexorable sand waves

On North Carolina's Outer Banks, sand waves moved westward across the land, blowing up the gently sloping northeast sides of the first small dunes to their crests. They continued to grow, higher than the woods behind them, until they were seventy- to ninety-foot mountains of sand covering hundreds of acres. Eventually they became so high that sand blew over them instead of accumulating at the peak, and the dunes traveled westward, burying live forests in front of them and exhuming dead ones previously covered. Today, all along the banks, you can see the stumps of cedars and oaks left behind the traveling dunes.

Although dunes worldwide come in a variety of basic shapes, including linear, star, dome, and parabolic, it is the simplest form—crescentic—that North America's traveling dunes take. This profile can move quickly—a group of dunes in China moved more than a hundred yards per year. Traveling dunes also have a secure place in history—the Wright Brothers experimented with their flying machines on the migrating hills at Kitty Hawk on the Outer Banks.

Sometimes the ebb and sway of traveling dunes offer surprises. When a storm in March 1846 tore away a line of dunes on the Outer Banks, it exposed a grove of dead junipers, which, with their "gigantic arms stretched impressively heavenward," were recognized by a local inhabitant. During the War of 1812, this man had hid in this same grove while boiling seawater for salt. The certainty of this was proven when he dug and found two of his three-by-six-foot pans where he had left them thirty-four years earlier just before the dunes buried them.

Traveling dunes are also found near Ipswich, Massachusetts, and on the north side of Long Island's south fork near Montauk, New York. The West Coast has an impressive region of mobile sand dunes at Oregon's Dunes Coast that extend for fifty miles south of Florence. These peaks reach three hundred feet and travel northeast as fast as sixteen feet per year, at points extending more than two miles from the sea. In some places the wind sculpts bowls and funnels around otherwise engulfed tall trees, creating little grottoes.

Traveling dunes sometimes give birth to another phenomenon: sunken forests. A famous example, only one-fifth of a square mile in area, exists on New York's Fire Island. This little tangle and dark glen of pitch pines, hollies, red maples, black tupelos, and sassafras trees is protected by the island's largest dunes, up to thirty feet in height. Other forests of this kind were found in Massachusetts and New Jersey; the town of Wildwood, New Jersey, is named for a similar forest. An early observer, after walking along the open beach and topping the rise above Fire Island's Sunken Forest, was taken with the scene: "For the tortured and wind-defaced growths already viewed hardly prepare us for that sense of repose, that vision of wild and savage luxuriance which, although still of a sand-beach character, now lies below us so widespread. . . ." A boardwalk nature trail winds through the only two- to three-century-old woods. But climbing the sand slope to enter the sunken forest reveals a peculiar sight—the top of the canopy of trees is even and equal in height with the surrounding dunes.

TROPICAL FISH STRAYS

Juvenile vagrancy is normal for some fish (but can also be fatal)

The highly mobile adults of the many species of fish that occur on the East Coast of North America travel to occupy waters with temperatures they are comfortable in as the seasons change. Because East Coast waters undergo such large changes in temperatures, many kinds of fish are forced to move long distances northward and southward to remain within their tolerances. But young tropical fish are an exception, and such movements may not be in their best interests.

Every spring and summer the Gulf Stream, that northerly flowing ribbon of warm water that tracks the East

Coast, carries untold numbers of newly spawned eggs and larvae of coral reef and other warmwater fish. These young fish transform to the juvenile stage—miniature adults—and then settle into bays and inlets inshore from the Gulf Stream all the way north to the Gulf of Maine.

If you snorkel and observe fish or pull a seine net through the sandy shallows of Barnegat Bay in New Jersey or Shinnecock Bay in Long Island, New York, you are likely to find young grouper, gray snapper, butterfly fish, trumpet-fish, trunkfish, lookdown, jacks, and a host of other kinds normally found in southern Florida and the Caribbean. Although the numbers may change, with particular years being strong for certain species, these tropical "exotics" are regular annual visitors to mid-Atlantic environs.

Some of these exotics are extremely exotic. In September 2001 my friend Todd Gardner, a maniacal collector of these fish, was snorkeling in Long Island's Fire Island Inlet. As he approached an old wooden piling, his knowledgeable eye saw an amazing sight. It was a tiny lionfish—a poisonous-spined species common in the Indo-Pacific and Indian Oceans. He managed to catch it in a dip net and later learned that a population of these appears to be established off North Carolina, which may have produced young that drifted north. It's not clear whether these fish colonized U.S. waters via aquarium releases (they are kept as pets) or by transport in the bilgewater of tankers.

Some exotics make it even farther north. A friend, Steve Stanne, was vacationing in central Maine and poking around the tide pools. He caught an incongruously bright little fish that he sketched. Later, the drawing showed clearly that it was a tropical butterfly fish—from the famously cold waters north of Cape Cod!

But after flourishing in these northern habitats in the semitropical warmth of summer, autumn's chill delivers a sad finale for many of these wanderers. The faster-swimming kinds may migrate south to avoid low water temperatures. Some individuals survive winter by moving into the warmwater discharges of electric-generation plants (if the plant shuts down temporarily, the fish perish). But based on divers' observations, the many, less mobile tropical fish die slow deaths on the bottom, unable to cope with the strange predicament nature arranged for them.

TSUNAMI

If you can see it, you're probably in trouble

To the uninitiated, there are few sights as harmless when looking from afar or as frightening up close as a tsunami. *Tsunami* (meaning "large waves in harbors" in Japanese) or tidal waves are not caused by the tide (or the wind), but by impulsive disturbances that displace water—earthquakes and especially seaquakes. These underwater earthquakes are the prime movers, but shakers also include landslides, volcanic eruptions, nuclear explosions, and even the impacts of large meteorites. Most tsunami occur in the seismically active Pacific basin; the Japanese are experts at dealing with tsunami, having experienced more than fifty over the last seventy-five years. But records of tsunami go back millennia and may have been responsible for biblical stories of the Flood and other inundations.

The eruption of Krakatoa near Sumatra in 1883 produced a well-documented, catastrophic tsunami. So loud was the volcano's largest explosion that it was heard in Madagascar, three thousand miles away. The resultant tsunami destroyed three hundred towns and villages, sank many ships, and killed 36,380 people.

Offshore, the waves of a tsunami are only a foot or two high and may be unnoticed from ships as they pass. But as they approach land, they slow down in shallow water and build up to gargantuan heights, striking with forces as strong as fifty tons per square yard. The approaching wave may sound a loud roar that sounds like a train or aircraft.

The first wave is often preceded by a sudden and extreme ebbing of sea from the shore. Typically they arrive in a series of eight waves, with the third and eighth being largest. And they may be spread far apart, with gaps between the waves of one hundred to six hundred miles, causing them to reach the shore fifteen minutes to an hour apart. Often, many of the deaths that occurred in tsunami were of people who went down to the shore after the first wave to investigate damage or pick up flopping fish, only to be caught in the next awesome rush. No one can outrun a tsunami; when you are near shore and see one approaching, it's already too late to flee. Elaborate education and warning systems are now in place around the Pacific Rim.

The highest tsunami recorded struck the North American coast near Valdez, Alaska—a remarkable 220 feet. A thirty-foot tsunami struck Oregon in 1700. The last great one on the West Coast originated from the "Good Friday Earthquake" of 1964, which killed 132 people in Alaska, of whom 122 died from the tsunami. It also claimed eleven people in California and swept away four children in Oregon who were camping on the beach. But don't wait around in sight of the shore hoping to see a tsunami, even from an ostensibly safe distance; between 479 B.C. and

1967 only 286 destructive-sized tsunami are known to have occurred.

∽∾∿

VAGRANT SEABIRDS
Blown sideways through life

Birds are the most mobile organisms on earth. But by spending time high up in the air where weather systems are ripping across, many become displaced from their normal ranges, some remarkably so. And their vagrancy does not go unnoticed. Not only are bird-watchers exquisitely keen observers, but they typically maintain "life lists" or records of every species they've seen; accomplished birders find it hard to add to their life lists in a given area unless they spot vagrants. When word goes out through the grapevine that a rare bird has been seen, birders shaking with excitement may flock from all over at the opportunity to see it and chalk up another species.

Indeed, when notice went out on the New York City Rare Bird Alert in August 1988 that a lone broad-billed sandpiper from across the Atlantic was at the Jamaica Bay Wildlife Refuge, hundreds of birders from as far as California rushed to the site, hoping to glimpse the drab, seven-inch-long alien. Rare shorebirds, such as curlew, American avocet, Hudsonian godwit, Wilson's phalarope, and whimbrel are recorded there almost every year; recently two new kinds of Siberian sandpipers were spotted.

Cape May, New Jersey, that coastal birding paradise, has of course hosted many an avian visitor from afar; it is such a good birding spot that the chances of sighting "accidentals"—birds far outside their normal ranges—are greater than elsewhere. The list recorded there includes black-browed albatross, South Polar skua, Eskimo curlew, sooty tern, magnificent frigate bird, whiskered tern from Africa, and a northern "Greenland" wheatear.

Theories abound to explain these anomalous movements. In December 1927 hundreds of northern lapwings—Eurasian shorebirds not known for long-distance migrations—showed up on the coasts of Labrador and Newfoundland. Apparently, to escape a sudden freeze, flocks of this species moved westward toward the milder coast, and then were entrained in easterlies that swept them toward North America. This phenomenon reoccurred in January 1966 when lapwings were sighted in New Brunswick, Nova Scotia, and Montauk, New York. Farther south it's likely that eastern trade winds are accountable for the appearances across the Atlantic of southern European birds such as the little egret.

Some shorebirds often considered to be North American actually breed both in northwestern Alaska and northeastern Siberia, in the vicinity of birds that winter in the Old World. Individuals of these Eurasian species may mistakenly associate with flocks of the North American kinds, wintering with them in the New World, thus providing frequent sightings.

Within North America, strong southwesterlies may direct birds well out of their ranges to the northeast. This may account for the appearance in 1983 on Nantucket of a western reef-heron, normally found in the southern Caribbean.

Another hypothesized mechanism for vagrancy is transport by transoceanic ships. But one seaman from the Cunard Lines kept notes on bird landings aboard his ships on about one hundred voyages. He found that although landings were not infrequent, almost all the birds departed within a few hours or died long before the vessel reached port.

∽∾∾

WATERSPOUTS

The "spin cycle" writ large

When a tornado passes over the sea, it's known as a waterspout, but these occurrences are rare. More common is a whirling wind funnel over water that develops in place during fair weather. But not under just any conditions—waterspouts are likeliest when cold humid air rides across warm water. I saw one whirl over New York Harbor in a freakish

storm that brought rain, sleet, and snowfall over still-tepid October waters—ideal waterspout conditions.

When a waterspout starts to form, typically a circular light-colored disc is centered within a larger dark area on the water's surface. Then light- and dark-colored surface bands begin to spiral from the dark spot, followed by a dense swirling ring of spray, but with an "eye," as seen in hurricanes. This evolves into a mature vortex that extends from the water surface to the overhead cloud mass and may rotate at up to two hundred miles per hour. The spray vortex can rise to a height of several hundred feet (the tallest waterspout ever recorded occurred off New South Wales, Australia, in 1898, and was nearly a mile high) and may leave a wake as it travels, at speeds of ten to fifteen knots. Waterspouts tend to last from two to twenty minutes before decaying.

Of course, any whirlwind that picks up water can also pick up what lives in it—many accounts of rains of fish and frogs occur in ancient literature. Recently, a waterspout struck coastal Oregon and deposited fish all over a highway in Lincoln City.

WAVES

Rippling bay or savage ocean

In her evocative essay, "Becoming Water," Susan Zwinger gave this instruction on how to begin such an apprenticeship: "Lie on a large log at the high-tide line by the ocean an hour before the highest high tide of the month. The waves will boom below human hearing. Take on the power of the incoming ocean in your bones."

Few forces in this world are as relentless as waves—it's estimated that eight thousand of them hammer an ocean beach every day. And they come in an endless array of sizes and forms. The most subtle wave is the descriptively named cat's paw. Whispers of wind test the surface tension of the water, producing arcing patterns of gently ruffled waves, often with a "paw" on the downwind side. On the other end of the scale are waves that crash over the tops of hundred-foot-tall lighthouses. Shorelines are carved by this relentless chiseling. A graphic example of the force of waves over time was provided on Maine's Matinicus Rock. There, a giant granite boulder, estimated to weigh one hundred tons, moved twelve feet during the lifetime of one of the island's lightkeepers. And the roar of breaking waves—what John Stilgoe called the *clamor nauticus*—can travel remarkably far; Charles Darwin reported that at South America's Tierra del Fuego after a heavy gale the surf could be heard at night a distance of "21 sea miles across a hilly and wooded country."

If you watch waves, you'll notice they are not all equal. Some say every seventh wave is the largest. Quite often big waves tend to come in threes. The average height of waves is a function of wind strength and duration, as well as fetch—the uninterrupted distance the wind can blow across the sea. Although average wave height is of concern to mariners and surfers, they also must pay attention to wave outliers—those rogues that far exceed the mean. Both statistical calculations and seamen's observations suggest that 1 wave in 23 is twice the average wave height; 1 wave in 1,175 is three times the average wave height; and 1 wave in 300,000 (which is the normal number a ship encounters during one month at sea) is four times the average wave height. Perhaps a more practical measure of the danger from waves is the significant wave height or "average worst," taken to be the average height of the highest one-third of all waves observed in a ten-minute period.

Waves can travel great distances—as much as five thousand miles. It is believed that some of the waves that approach the California coast from the south begin in storms off New Zealand. Many of the waves breaking on North America's East Coast begin south of Greenland and east of Newfoundland in a storm center of the North Atlantic. But the trained eye can distinguish between waves born long ago and those that are freshly sprung. "Old" waves or "swells" that have traveled long distances are broader, but they rear up in the surf zone, curl forward, and break hard. Newly birthed waves tend to have a more peaked shape, spilling scuds of foam down their steeper slopes.

The Beaufort Wind Force Scale to classify wind force at sea was devised in 1805 by Admiral Sir Francis Beaufort. The original scheme made no reference to the speed of the wind; wind speeds in knots were added during the twentieth century. Although it's not often used by meteorologists today, it still gives a useful perspective on the relationship between wind and wave.

Beaufort Number	Wind	Wind Speed (knots)	Description of Sea Surface
0	Calm	less than 1	Sea like a mirror
1	Light air	1–3	Ripples like scales
2	Light breeze	4–6	Small wavelets
3	Gentle breeze	7–10	Large wavelets
4	Moderate breeze	11–16	Small waves
5	Fresh breeze	17–21	Moderate waves
6	Strong breeze	22–27	Large waves
7	Moderate gale	28–33	Sea heaps up
8	Fresh gale	34–40	Moderately high waves
9	Strong gale	41–47	High waves
10	Whole gale	48–55	Very high waves
11	Storm	56–63	Exceptionally high waves
12	Hurricane	64+	Air completely filled with foam and spray

It's not difficult to predict the average height of waves in a gale, assuming you know the dimensions of the storm and the water body it's blowing across. Simply multiply one and a half times the square root of the fetch. If a bay is a hundred miles wide, then fifteen-foot waves are to be expected. Waves break when the bottom of the wave "feels" the seafloor, most typically along a beach. This breaking and tumbling of waves begins when the ratio of wave height to water depth reaches 4:3.

Waves streaming offshore at an angle normally refract, or bend, to become nearly parallel to the shore as they strike a beach. One exception is a beach in California near La Jolla where the unusual underwater topography causes them to come in fast and sideways to the shore—the beach and its waves are called "The Freaks." A little north, in Monterey at Point Joe, a rough seabed causes surface currents and waves to boil and bubble so out of proportion to prevailing conditions that the area is called "The Restless Sea." Oregon has a similar site at Cape Perpetua called the "Devil's Churn."

Large waves that strike the shore sometimes climb higher because of "spouting." Spouting takes place when the plunging mass of water traps a pocket of air against an unyielding surface such as a cliff or lighthouse, compresses it, and then is flung skyward by the air's explosive reexpansion. Another rock formation called a "sea horn" at Oregon's Depoe Bay spouts water as much as a hundred feet in the air.

Waves also climb higher occasionally in places with unusual topography where they look tame, or at least manageable, but then strike the unwary. The stark, almost moonlike rocky landscape of Peggy's Cove, Nova Scotia, attracts thousands of tourists. But when the surf is rough, great waves sometimes roll up a bedrock cut called the "funnel"; several unsuspecting victims have been swept to sea there. At Duncan's Point, at California's Sonoma Coast Beaches State

Park, no less than twenty-one people have been washed off, with not a single body found. One theory is that crests from different storms sometimes meet and combine here, and when closely aligned merge to create occasional outlandishly large waves. A barbed-wire fence has ended these losses.

Rogue waves are poorly understood terrors, great mountains of water that are the sum of smaller waves. These anomalous waves may be 60 to 80 feet in height; in 1933, while sailing in a storm in the South Pacific, a U.S. Navy tanker survived the largest wave ever measured, 112 feet high. The Gloucester fishing vessel *Andrea Gail* and its six crew members chronicled in Sebastian Junger's *The Perfect Storm* fell victim in a raging nor'easter to a wave estimated at more than a hundred feet high.

Despite the damage that waves can cause, they are also a source of great pleasure. Wyman Richardson wrote of those August and September days on Cape Cod when hurricanes passed hundreds of miles offshore, generating a surf that he could hear a mile away. He described the scene from a bluff:

Wave after wave, in stately majesty, comes rolling slowly and irresistibly toward the shore. On the outer bar the water piles up in a veritable mountain, and, as the crest topples over in a mass of white foam, the illusion of a snow-capped mountain peak becomes even more striking. As the water shoals up, steeper and higher become the waves. Their backs begin to hump up and curve away in an easy slope to to the following trough, while the forward wall becomes more and more concave. Eagerly, the top of the wave rushes on while the foot, in its struggle with the friction of the sandy bottom, is more and more slowed up. The suspense is almost unbearable, as for one breath-taking moment the wave seems to hang in mid-air. Then comes a deafening crash, which

shakes the beach, and a smother of white foam leaps high
into the sky as if to snatch at the sun.

And of course, few segments of society enjoy waves as in-
timately as surfers do—word spreads quickly and little else
matters when there are perfectly breaking seas. One of the
most unusual surfing sites is under the Golden Gate Bridge,
where large waves hurtle past the bridge's stanchions. But
even wave-savvy surfers misjudge these forces—I once witnessed an ambulance race to Point Judith, Rhode Island,
where a surfer slammed face-first into a barnacle-covered
rock. Although lucky to be alive, his features were barely visible through the blood, cuts, and bruises.

Waves also are what produces *mal de mer* or seasickness,
a remarkably miserable state that causes captains to watch
badly stricken victims for signs of suicide. Seasickness is
said to cause two great fears: first, that you're going to die,
and second, that you won't die.

〰️

WHALE STRANDINGS
Sad, mysterious, and usually irreversible

Aristotle, writing in his treatise *Historia Animalium*
more than two thousand years ago, mentioned whale
strandings on the shores of the Mediterranean Sea, noting,
"It is not known for what reason they run themselves
aground on dry land." A couple of millennia later it still is
not definitively known. But several reasonable explanations have been advanced.

One theory involves a failure of the whales' echolocation systems in the shallows. In addition to the other "standard" senses, whales perceive their surroundings by
emitting sounds that are echoed in the ocean medium and

then received. Much like bats in the air, whales use this endowment to find prey and avoid obstacles. But on a gently sloping seafloor, the increasing shallowness toward shore is so gradual that the whale's echolocation system may not detect marked changes—leaving it vulnerable to stranding. It's also possible that disease or parasites interfere with echolocation. Other theories include extreme social cohesion where one sick animal is followed to shore by healthy peers, and harrassment by predators or humans.

Not all whales are prone to these episodes. Baleen whales rarely strand; the whales prone to this behavior are toothed whales, normally found well offshore, such as pilot whales, false killer whales, and sperm whales.

One seaman told Thoreau that the frequent strandings of pilot whales on Cape Cod happened when they chased squid toward shore. Pilot whales, known as "blackfish" in his time, were an important part of the Cape Cod economy. When herds were spotted offshore, small boats were launched to steer them toward the shallows, or to lance them in the deep if they didn't cooperate. But sometimes early risers had a far easier time of it, discovering and claiming large pods of blackfish that had beached themselves overnight.

When apparently healthy whales strand and can't be returned to the sea, their predicament is heartbreaking. In *A Presentation of Whales,* Barry Lopez wrote of an incident that occurred in Oregon when a herd of sperm whales became stranded on a remote section of beach, where "They lay on the western shore of North America like forty-one derailed boxcars." This fourth largest sperm whale stranding in recorded history attracted marine scientists, federal and state agency representatives, reporters, and thousands of the interested public composed of everyone from drunkards who found it entertaining to people who whispered as if at a funeral or sat in religious stances. With no way to save them, veterinarians were called in to try to give them lethal injections, but even this humane gesture wasn't effective. The whales died on their own from heat and suffocation, the last one expiring thirty-six hours after it rode up on the beach.

Some whales perish at sea from natural or unnatural causes. Whales that die and then sink to the bottom in the ocean depths serve as important food sources for unique communities of organisms that have evolved to capitalize on them. Researchers found that hagfish, sharks, and crabs reduce each body to bones within four months, but microorganisms persist much longer.

Occasionally, a floating whale corpse is picked up accidentally by a large seagoing tanker when the animal wraps around the bow, captain and crew unaware. I saw an adult finback whale being towed from the shipyards in New York Harbor where the dead whale had risen to the surface after the vessel docked. In 2001 there was considerable controversy as an unusually large number of whales were struck by ships in the busy lanes leading to New York Harbor; it's not clear how many, if any, of these whales were already dead from other causes. And in 1987 and 1988 twelve hundred dead dolphins washed up between New Jersey and Florida; these deaths may have been *Pfiesteria* related (see page 121).

When dead whales wash up on shore, they become an awe-inspiring attraction. And with so much flesh rotting, they also produce stupefying stenches. But disposing of such a giant carcass is no easy task. The ultimate whale-removal episode occurred on the shore near Florence, Oregon, in November 1970. The aroma from a forty-five-foot fin whale had so bothered local residents that the Oregon State Highway Division was called in to do something.

None of the workers wanted to cut up the putrid mass, and they were concerned that if they buried it in place, the surf might wash it out again. So it was decided to blast it into small pieces that gulls and other scavengers could eat. The behemoth's sides were lined with half a ton of dynamite. A crowd gathered to watch at a supposedly safe distance a quarter mile away. Fortunately, a television crew filmed the explosion and aftermath—and this footage is now something of a cult classic.

The explosion is mammoth on film. You can hear members of the delighted crowd saying "whee!" and "ohhhh!" at its sight and "Fred, you can take your hands out of your ears." But then the mood changes as someone shouts "here come the pieces" and "ow" as the microphone picks up the soft *blop* sounds of whale chunks falling like rain on the crowd.

Later, the news crew provided this voice-over: "Our camera stopped rolling shortly after the blast. The humor of the entire situation suddenly gave way to a run for survival as huge chunks of whale blubber fell everywhere. Pieces of meat passed high over our heads while others were falling at our feet. The dunes were rapidly evacuated as spectators escaped both the falling debris and overwhelming smell."

Although no one was hurt, no one went home without a coating of whale particles. And a car parked a quarter mile away was crushed by a large whale slab. In the end the remaining chunks were too large to be eaten by the gulls, which had either been scared off by the explosion or kept away by the odor.

❧

WHALE-, DOLPHIN-, AND PORPOISE-WATCHING
Leviathans ahead!

It's hard to know who is watching whom when humans observe the highly intelligent cetaceans—whales, dolphins, and porpoises. Often as people hang over a boat's rails in rapture at their sight, the whales roll to their sides and look back, or "spyhop," by rising vertically partway out of the water to survey the scene.

Whale-watching, the blanket term for observing the whole cetacean clan, has become a big business on all of North America's shores since it began in 1955 at San Diego, California. In 1998 more than five million eager watchers jumped on tour boats to be taken to the whale grounds. And the likelihood of spotting them is high; by running trips almost continuously, speaking with other vessels in the area, and even employing spotter planes, a close tab can be kept on whales' positions.

My family and I once boarded a tour boat run from Grand Manan Island at the mouth of the Bay of Fundy. As we ran over the food-rich green waters, life was evident all around us, with storm petrels, gulls, terns, and even puffins gathering near the boat as a narrator told us what to expect. Soon we were near the mouth of the great bay, and humpback whales were all around us. The captain cut the engine so as not to spook the whales, and for the next three hours we were in the midst of a large clan of breaching whales, at times within fifty feet of the boat. All of the passengers returned to the dock elated at a spectacular session.

Although the tours have a high batting average, no whale-watch operator bats a thousand. On another tour we took in the Canadian Maritimes, many of the children on board spent the hours vomiting in the rough seas, not a single whale was sighted, and the trip's high point was our spotting a bald eagle in a tree on shore that we could have seen from the dock.

The targets of these tours range from the truly leviathan, such as the blue whale that can surpass a hundred feet and two hundred tons and has a heart as large as a compact car, to sleek, playful dolphins about the size of a person. In between there are dozens of species of a great variety of sizes, forms, and habits. Among them are right whales—*right* because early whalers considered it the right whale to catch, since it floated when killed, no minor detail in those days when whales were handled with brawn and hand tools. Only about three hundred right whales are left in the western North Atlantic. The finback whale is the world's only asymmetrically pigmented mammal—the left side of the head and jaw is dark, the right side light. This feature may have to do with herding prey fish such as herring: A whale circles around the school to the right, showing its less visible light side. Starkly black-and-white-patterned killer whales or orcas hunt Pacific waters in packs for seals and sea otters. And on the Gulf of Mexico coast, porpoises are often seen breaching just outside the surf line.

Binoculars help you look for key characteristics in identifying species from long distances. Among these features are the shape and height of the spout when a whale exhales, the presence of a fin on its back, whether it spyhops, its length, whether it has markings or barnacles on it, and whether it has true teeth (sixty-six species worldwide) or plankton-straining baleen (ten species).

Along the North Atlantic coast, whale-watch trips are offered in many coastal towns from Newfoundland to New York. Quebec alone has more than fifty boats operating near the confluence of the St. Lawrence and Saguenay Rivers, a location that has its own population of beluga whales. South of New York the numbers of tour operators are less and many focus on dolphin-watching, due to a scarcity of larger cetaceans. Hilton Head Island, South Carolina, has at least eight dolphin-watching enterprises. These well-observed animals are identified by characteristics of their dorsal fins, and have had terribly cute names bestowed on them, such as Dolly, Rambo, and Freckles.

California is the whale-watching capital of North America, with more than sixty-five operators and 140 boats in service. Trips to view blue and humpback whales are longer and more expensive than for the coast-hugging gray whales. Between Oregon and Alaska, many whale-watch tours are offered, focusing mainly on gray whales and orcas.

Whales are sometimes visible from shore. Although this occurred more frequently centuries ago when whales were numerous, at times they still can be seen, especially from high vantages such as cliffs in the Canadian Maritimes, and even from the south-side bluffs at Montauk, New York. Humpback whales have been spotted north of the Chesapeake Bay Bridge in recent years, near the mouth of the Chester River. Dolphins and porpoises often swim in nearshore waters. Bottlenose dolphins may be found all over the Chesapeake Bay, even far up the Potomac River near Washington, D.C.

Each year more than twenty thousand gray whales migrate from Alaska to Baja California along shallow waters off Washington, Oregon, and California, traveling south to calve in the warm lagoons of Mexico's coast and north to summer feeding grounds. This annual seven-thousand-mile trip at a rate of about a hundred miles per day takes eight to ten weeks each way. Such a lengthy journey provides many locations where the whales can be seen, even from shore, especially at coastal cliffs. Gray whales typically execute a regular diving–breathing sequence, which provides some guidance for whale-watchers as to where to look next. From three to five successive spouts usually signal a dive that covers about a thousand feet of horizontal distance in about three to four minutes.

It's hard to be a private whale in California. From the glassed-in observatory in San Diego's Cabrillo National Monument high on Point Loma (the first public whale-watch lookout), as many as two hundred whales per day have been spotted. Other good promontories for viewing parading gray whales include Point La Jolla, Dana Point, Point Fermin, Point Dume, Monterey, San Francisco's Farallon Islands, and Point Reyes National Seashore. And there are at least nine major gray whale festivals among California shore communities. California also offers resident herds of pilot whales, orcas, humpback whales, dolphins, and porpoises off the Channel Islands, Monterey Peninsula, and the northern coast.

Aptly named Cape Lookout in Oregon, which juts two miles into the ocean, is a premier whale-watching site where hikers at its tip can spy up to thirty whales per hour. The season for southerly migrating whales is December through March; returnees can be spotted from April through June. But the peak period is the last week of the year; at this time volunteers set up WHALE-WATCHING SPOKEN HERE signs at high viewpoints all along the Oregon coast where they wait to help visitors spot whales. They also can be seen from Vancouver's old White Rock Pier and Vancouver Island's Long Beach near Tofino.

About two hundred killer whales eat salmon and patrol the waters of Johnstone Strait between Vancouver Island and mainland British Columbia. They are an unusual matriarchical herd made up of mothers and sons and daughters that remain with them even as adults. East Point on the Strait of Georgia also is a great killer-whale-viewing location. Pacific white-sided dolphins have also shown recently at Johnstone Strait, in herds of as many as four hundred individuals.

It's not unusual on whale-watching trips to spot a whale-sized fish, either the whale shark—a true shark, not a whale—or the basking shark. Once as I sat on a whale-watch boat among a pod of right whales near the mouth of the Bay of Fundy, a basking shark more than twenty feet long swam by at the surface, also enjoying the rich feeding grounds. Basking sharks are the second largest fish in the world, reaching thirty feet; the largest is the whale shark, which can measure sixty feet. As do many whales, they reach these great sizes by filtering the seas for tiny plankton. Both are cosmopolitan and may be found almost anywhere along North America's temperate coastlines.

WHIRLPOOLS
You may have to row uphill

In a few places along North America's coastlines, particularly at higher latitudes where tidal ranges are greater, waters plunge through rock channels that generate whirlpools. Some are small and simply interesting to look at, but others are grand enough to be dangerous to swimmers and boaters. One of the best known is also the largest in the Western Hemisphere: Old Sow Whirlpool, in the western passage of

Passamaquoddy Bay, between Deer Island, New Brunswick, and Moose Island, near Eastport, Maine.

The passage that includes Old Sow Whirlpool comes alive on each incoming or ebbing tide; these tides reverse by twenty-eight to thirty feet in height every six hours. The main whirlpool, which is about fifty feet in diameter, is unpredictable in its formation. When the flow is exceptionally strong because of winds or moon phase, not only will the waters whirl but in one section currents may also blast up from the bottom and spout several feet.

New York City once had comparable waters, the East River's famed Hell Gate, a gauntlet of reefs and ten-knot currents that grounded a thousand ships per year. So fierce were its whirlpools and rips that sailors could hear it fifteen minutes away. It was largely tamed in the late 1800s by a combination of excavation and dynamiting, however; one blast in 1885 used six times more dynamite than had ever been fired in the world, which sent geysers 250 feet high and may have been the biggest explosion prior to the atomic bomb.

The West Coast waters offering the perils nearest to those of Old Sow may be the Skookumchuck Rapids at Egmont, British Columbia. This foaming white-water tidal cataract puts on a spectacular show, which may include "extreme" kayakers cavorting on it. So powerful is the flow that in the old days children playing near the "Skook" were tied to trees for their safety.

Contrary to popular opinion, whirlpools do not conform to the direction of hemispheric Coriolis forces; they are instead much more influenced by the particular characteristics of currents and topography. (Nor is it true that toilets upon flushing swirl in opposite directions on either side of the equator—the direction depends on the characteristics of the bowl.)

Whirlpools are really large drains and thus are lower than the surrounding waters. A local Old Sow legend tells of a fisherman in a dinghy who got caught in the spinning circle. His response? "I didn't mind so much gettin' caught in it. What I resented was havin' to row uphill to get out!"

WIND TIDES

Even water has friction

In some places, such as the shallow sounds named Currituck, Albemarle, and Pamlico behind Hatteras Beach in North Carolina, the inlets allow some mixing with seawater, but not enough to create tidal variations. Yet water levels may change dramatically, simply due to wind. Fresh southwesters can cause a six- or eight-foot rise behind Oregon Inlet, and strong easterlies expose miles of sand flats in the same reaches.

The leading edges of hurricanes, which force great amounts of ocean waters into these sounds, can with their easterly winds lay bare the sand flats on the west side of the Outer Banks. But this is not a safe situation to be in. After the eye of the hurricane passes, the winds rip out of the west—pushing the accumulated water from the eastern side back like a tidal wave toward the banks, sometimes with such force that new inlets across the strand have been opened.

∽∾∽

WORM HATCHES
Not-so-beautiful swimmers

In summer, swimmers may be horrified and anglers thrilled to find swarms of short red worms swirling through the shallows. Although they don't bite, hordes of bristly reddish creatures with threatening-looking chitinous pincer jaws scare all but the bravest bathers. But fishermen know that these one- to two-inch forms of that common fish bait the sandworm are irresistible to striped bass and other gamefish.

Worm hatches occur during the time of the full and new moons, usually between two and three days on each side, from about May through September. In a worm hatch, millions of specialized reproductive stages of the sandworm find each other via chemical stimuli. Writhing near the water surface, females shed their eggs in a puff and males release their sperm. So many may come together that the water feels slimy and smells fishy.

In some parts of the world, such as Pacific islands that lack for protein, when hatches of worms happen, islanders take off from work, scoop up worms, and have a great feast. In the United States only anglers, particularly fly fishermen, enthusiastically anticipate these hatches. Special red flies are tied to "match the hatch," and these are often the only lures that cause stripers to strike as they gorge on the easy-to-catch worms. Some fishing guides specialize in this form of fishing, especially in the coastal salt ponds of Rhode Island.

For all at least return to the sea—to Oceanus, the ocean river, like the ever-flowing stream of time, the beginning and the end.

—Rachel Carson
The Sea Around Us